The Greek
Epic Cycle

Current and forthcoming titles in the Bristol Classical Paperbacks series:

Alexander the Great: King, Commander and Statesman, N. Hammond
Art of the Aeneid, W. Anderson
Art of the Odyssey, H. Clarke
Athenian Democracy in the Age of Demosthenes, M.H. Hansen
Catullan Revolution, K. Quinn
Cicero: A Portrait, E. Rawson
Criticism in Antiquity, D. Russell
Epyllion from Theocritus to Ovid, M. Crump
Euripides & Dionysus: an interpretation of the Bacchae,
    R. Winnington-Ingram
Georgics of Virgil, L. Wilkinson
The Greek Epic Cycle, M. Davies
The Greek Way of Death, R. Garland
Herodotus, J. Gould
Historians of Greece and Rome, S. Usher
History of Cynicism, D. Dudley
History of Sparta, W. Forrest
Horace and his Lyric Poetry, L. Wilkinson
Imagery and Poetry of Lucretius, D. West
Latin Poets and Roman Life, J. Griffin
Law of Athens (2 vols.), A. Harrison
Livy: His Historical Aims and Methods, P. Walsh
Magic, Reason and Experience, G. Lloyd
Neoplatonism, R. Wallis
The Piraeus, R. Garland
Plutarch, D. Russell
Poet Lucan, M. Morford
Political Background of Aeschylean Tragedy, A. Podlecki
Presocratics, E. Hussey
Propertius, M. Hubbard
Roman Novel, P. Walsh
Roman Poetry & Propaganda in the Age of Augustus, A. Powell (ed.)
Roman Satire, M. Coffey
Rome: Its People, Life and Customs, U. Paoli
Satires of Horace, N. Rudd
Satires of Persius, C. Dessen
Science, Folklore and Ideology, G. Lloyd
Stoics, F. Sandbach
Story of the Iliad, E. Owen
Suetonius, A. Wallace-Hadrill
Tacitus, R. Martin
Themes in Roman Satire, N. Rudd
Three Archaic Poets: Archilochus, Alcaeus, Sappho, A. Pippin Burnett
Virgil's Epic Technique, R. Heinze (tr. H. & D. Harvey & F. Robertson)
Wild Justice, J. Mossman
Women in Greek Myth, M. Lefkowitz
Xenophon, J. Anderson

THE GREEK EPIC CYCLE

Malcolm Davies

This impression 2003
First published in 1989 by
Bristol Classical Press
an imprint of
Gerald Duckworth & Co. Ltd.
90-93 Cowcross Street, London EC1M 6BF
Tel: 020 7490 7300
Fax: 020 7490 0080
inquiries@duckworth-publishers.co.uk
www.ducknet.co.uk

© 1989 by Malcolm Davies

All rights reserved. No part of this publication
may be reproduced, stored in a retrieval system, or
transmitted, in any form or by any means, electronic,
mechanical, photocopying, recording or otherwise,
without the prior permission of the publisher.

A catalogue record for this book is available
from the British Library

ISBN 1 85399 039 6

Contents

Preface	vi
Abbreviations	viii
1. The Epic Cycle	1
Notes	11
2. The Titanomachy	13
3. The Oedipodeia	19
4. The Thebais	22
5. The Epigoni	29
6. The Cypria	32
7. The Aethiopis	51
8. The Little Iliad	60
9. The Sack of Troy	71
10. The Returns Home	77
11. The Telegony	84
Index of Mythological Names	92

Preface

This little book is a pendant to the first part of my *Epicorum Graecorum Fragmenta* published in 1988 by Vandenhoeck and Ruprecht. It contains a literal English translation of those fragments of the Epic Cycle there edited which are directly quoted by ancient authors. It also contains a résumé of the import of those fragments which are not verbal quotations; a paraphrase of Proclus' prose summary of the contents of the Trojan epics within the cycle; and a very brief commentary on fragments and prose summary. Perhaps this scheme needs some justification.

Why, for instance, publish literal translations of those tiny portions of confessedly second-rate epics that happen to have survived? Partly, I suppose, because less literal translations that hide their originals' shortcomings can themselves be misleading. To take one example: Iona and Peter Opie, at the start of their fascinating book *The Singing Game* (Oxford 1985), observe (p. 4): 'Another ancient circular dance was that in which a leader stood in the centre of the ring and sang the verse, and the ring acted as chorus. This seems to be described in the *Titanomachy*.' The warrant for this important inference is T.F. Higham's over-enthusiastic rendering of F 5 in the *Oxford Book of Greek Verse in Translation*, p. 180:

> Himself, the sire of men, of gods the sire,
> The centre took, and led the dancing quire.

Unfortunately, as a brisk look at my own literal translation (p. 15) of the one-line fragment will confirm, practically the whole of the second verse of Higham's translation is of his own devising. And even more unfortunately, it is on this portion of the translation that the Opies' picture of a leader in the centre of the ring, singing to an accompanying chorus, is based. Perhaps literal translations do have their uses.

My 'very brief commentary on fragments and Proclus' prose summary' needs even more urgent justification in a sense, since it abounds in controversial statements that ideally require far more in the way of substantiation than they receive here. My excuse must be that in fact they will receive exactly such justification in the far more detailed commentaries that will be published by Vandenhoeck and Ruprecht in the coming years. But it was put to me that a certain class of reader might positively prefer the greatly simplified summary of what I think we know about these poems that they will find here. Everyone can be referred to the more scholarly and circumspect treatments shortly to appear, though not everyone will need all the information. Interest in the Epic Cycle has never been stronger, whether on the part of people concerned with Greek myth from the literary or artistic viewpoint or of people impressed by the light that can be thrown on Homer's art by comparison and contrast. A short statement of the salient points and the inferences that have been drawn from the data at our disposal can do no harm and may be found useful.

When composing the commentaries referred to above, I necessarily learned much from the writings of earlier scholars. Their names will be found amid the ample documentation in the relevant volumes. With the exception of the Introduction, I have not thought it appropriate to include such doxography here. Likewise, there already exists a number of literal translations of fragments of the Epic Cycle into English. At the time of writing my commentaries, I consulted these and doubtless learned much. But I did not trouble to refresh my memory as to their renderings when I produced the translations found in the present volume. It would be disingenuous to suppose that what I once read has not sometimes influenced my own choice of word or phrase, however unconsciously, but I decided to leave the issue at that and make no further investigation.

Before closing I must thank Kim Richardson of Bristol Classical Press for providing the first impulse towards the production of this volume and for help and encouragement since.

Malcolm Davies
St. John's College, Oxford

Abbreviations

Angular brackets contain information that is easily inferred but not actually present in the passage translated or paraphrased.

Fragments and Testimonia of early Greek epic are cited ('F' and 'T') by the numeration of my *Epicorum Graecorum Fragmenta* (*E.G.F.*, Göttingen 1988). Other fragmentary authors are cited as follows:

DK: Diels and Kranz, *Die Fragmente der Vorsokratiker*[8] (Berlin 1952).

F.Gr.Hist.: *Die Fragmente der Griechischen Historiker* ed. F. Jacoby.

LP: Lobel and Page, *Poetarum Lesbiorum Fragmenta* (Oxford 1955).

MW: Merkelbach and West, *Fragmenta Hesiodea* (Oxford 1967).

P: D.L. Page, *Poetae Melici Graeci* (Oxford 1962).

Pf: R. Pfeiffer, *Callimachi Fragmenta* (Oxford 1949).

Sn: B. Snell, *Pindari Fragmenta*[4] (Leipzig 1975).

Tr.G.F.: *Tragicorum Graecorum Fragmenta*
vol. 2 (Göttingen 1981) *Adespota* ed. Snell and Kannicht.
vol. 3 (Göttingen 1985) *Aeschylus* ed. S.L. Radt.
vol. 4 (Göttingen 1977) *Sophocles* ed. S.L. Radt.

W: B. Wyss, *Antimachi Colophonii Reliquiae* (Berlin 1936).

Wehrli: *Die Schule des Aristoteles* ed. F. Wehrli.

1: The Epic Cycle

The second-century AD writer Athenaeus presents (in his rambling monograph *Deipnosophistae* or *A Banquet of Learning*) a number of anecdotes about the Greek tragedian Sophocles, including the rather scandalous story of his successful ploy to kiss a beautiful youth serving wine at a banquet (Athen. 603^E).[1] A somewhat more edifying tradition[2] preserved by the same author is that 'Sophocles took great pleasure in the Epic Cycle and composed whole dramas in which he followed the Cycle's version of myths' (277^C). What was this Epic Cycle that meant so much to Sophocles? Should it mean very much (if anything) to us?

Definition[3]

In fact Athenaeus' account is (pedantically considered) a little misleading since there is no real evidence that the term 'Epic Cycle' as such would have meant anything to Sophocles. Our earliest extant allusion to the existence of the Epic Cycle occurs in a work of Aristotle (*Anal. Post.* 1.12 (77^B 32 = *T 2) though the interpretation of the relevant phrase has been questioned. If the allusion is correctly detected, Aristotle's reference implies that the 'Eristics' (a group of philosophers responsible for the Sophistic fallacies Aristotle is attacking) attributed to Homer a cycle of epics. Several of the poems in the Epic Cycle as we now know it were attributed to (among others) Homer (in particular the *Thebais* (see p. 22) and the *Cypria* (see p. 32)) and other early epics besides (e.g. the *Oechalias Halosis* or *Sack of Oechalia*: E.G.F. pp. 149ff.) so it is easy to believe that this is what Aristotle means.

It is, however, with the Alexandrian scholars that we first meet with an interest in the Epic Cycle which is at all widely and reliably attested. The term 'cyclic' was used by them not only to refer in a relatively factual manner to the composers and contents of the Cycle's epics but also in a more subjective and denigratory way that emphasised the great difference in poetic quality between these poets and Homer (see below, p. 9). That difference had already been stressed by Aristotle in his *Poetics* (see below p. 8) where, even though he does not specifically use the terms 'Cycle' or 'cyclic', he draws attention to the lack of unity in a poem such as the *Little Iliad* in contrast to the *Iliad* or *Odyssey*. The Alexandrian scholars inherited this distinction. They must also have edited the epics in question, as they edited most other works of Greek literature, though we know little of this edition except for the number of books into which each epic was divided.[4] Some evidence seems to suggest the existence of a 'cyclic edition' of the *Odyssey* and, perhaps, of the *Iliad*, wherein, presumably, the Homeric text was somehow adjusted to fit with the poems of the Epic Cycle that preceded or succeeded the *Iliad* and *Odyssey*. This is not to infer (what some have supposed) the existence of an edition of the Epic Cycle which achieved total consistency and continuity by the drastic expedient of excising whole chunks of poetry that happened to involve duplication or to produce contradiction of other passages within the Cycle. What the Alexandrian editors did was merely to edit a group of epic poems whose relatively early date, subject-matter and style had previously led to their being largely attributed to the author of the *Iliad* and *Odyssey*. The Alexandrians (like Aristotle before them) recognised that in many significant ways (see below p. 4) these poems were deeply unHomeric. Nevertheless the epics were to prove handy source-material to later writers of mythological hand-books because of their convenient (if uninspired) encapsulation of large chunks of myth. If Athenaeus is to be believed (above, p. 1), the individual poems which in the eyes of Aristotle and the Alexandrian editors constituted the Epic Cycle had already proved a useful quarry for plot-material in the case of Sophocles' tragedies.

Date

The epics in question have largely disappeared,[5] but fragments of them survive in the form of direct quotations or indirect references in the works of later writers. The directly quoted fragments are never very large, but even the relatively narrow band of evidence they supply presents fairly conclusive proof that, in comparison with Homer, there are linguistic forms that are 'late' and post-Homeric.[6] The first scholar adequately to stress this was the great German classicist Wilamowitz in 1884.[7] Following in his footsteps, J. Wackernagel, a distinguished philologist, published (some time after the start of the twentieth century) a fuller and more rigorous account of the evidence.[8] After rightly emphasising that the 'Konstanz des Stils' was greater in epic than any other genre of Greek literature, he proceeded to show that while the fragments of the *Thebais* and *Sack of Troy* contain almost nothing that is linguistically post-Homeric (this is consistent with the remarkably vigorous tradition that attributes the former to Homer (see below, p. 22)), the *Cypria* and the *Little Iliad* contain a good many such features.[9] F 1 of the *Cypria* is particularly rich in them, some of them without parallel before the fifth century, some of them Attic in form. Since F 1 of the *Cypria* seems to be part of a proem to the work as a whole (below, p. 33) Wackernagel concluded that it can hardly be dismissed as a later addition and consequently assigned the whole of the *Cypria* to an Attic context not long before 500 BC.

It is customary for scholars to make a nod of respect in Wackernagel's direction and then on the whole shy away from his radical late dating of the *Cypria* in particular and some of the Epic Cycle in general.[10] It may be felt that a dating of the *Cypria* almost a quarter of a century after the birth of Aeschylus and barely a decade before the birth of Sophocles is unacceptably late, especially if those dramatists were influenced by poems of the Epic Cycle (see p. 2). There may also be a vaguer feeling that by 500 BC the 'Age of Epic' should have long ago and decisively been replaced by the 'Age of Lyric'.[11] But this late dating fits very well with a recent placing of the Hesiodic *Catalogue of Women* in an Attic ambience of c.560-20 BC,[12] and relatively solid linguistic data must outweigh relatively flimsy feelings of propriety. The *Cypria*, indeed, may well be a special case: its main function as a hold-all for the complete story of the Trojan War up to the events of the *Iliad* suggest that its proem might well be the very latest and last element of the whole, an attempt to give the pre-existing epic a rather spurious unity (see below, p. 33). But the lack of unity of these epics as a whole (see p. 8), and their status as attempts to fill in the gaps left by Homer's poems, make me very reluctant to date most of them before the second half of the sixth century.

Aristarchus of Samothrace, the greatest of the Alexandrian scholars, certainly regarded these poems as 'late' relative to Homer.[13] Numerous Homeric scholia and other late writings reveal the traces of his approach: a mythical tradition not mentioned by Homer is deemed to have been unknown to Homer, and those authors who do mention the tradition are called *neóteroi* ('relatively recent'). Often these *neóteroi* can be shown to be equivalent to poets of the Epic Cycle.[14]

But a problem remains. Aristarchus' approach would seem to have been too schematic. Homer may have known many traditions which he does not specifically mention (he may be practising a deliberate reticence with some of them (below p. 8)). Often, besides, his way of telling a story seems to be modelled on another story which he does not actually mention: for instance, in *Il.* 8.130ff. it looks as if Antilochus' rescue of his father Nestor from Hector's onslaught may be based on his rescue (at the cost of his own life) of the same warrior from the Aethiopian prince Memnon, a tale we know to have featured in the cyclic epic the *Aethiopis* (see below, p. 53-4). Or again, in *Il.* 23.708ff. Odysseus' victory over Telamonian Ajax in the wrestling contest at the Funeral Games of Patroclus reminds one of Odysseus' victory over the same hero (at the cost of the latter's life) in the contest for the arms of Achilles, a tale we know to have featured in both *Aethiopis* and *Little Iliad* (see below, pp. 57 and 61ff.). There are various ways of explaining these parallels. The fullest and most detailed book to consider the question[15] arrives at a simple (some might allege simplistic) answer: Homer in each case was drawing on the relevant poem from the Epic Cycle. But this theory swiftly encounters an obstacle: precisely those post-Homeric linguistic forms mentioned above. The theory can, however, be re-cast to cope with this objection and escape an equivalent charge of schematism to that levelled above at Aristarchus. Provided we do not envisage Homer 'drawing on' specific *texts* of the *Aethiopis* or *Little Iliad* (least of all those texts from which our fragments with their post-Homeric linguistic forms derive) all will be well: Homer will have been acquainted with the stories of the deaths of Antilochus and Ajax when he composed the relevant parts of the *Iliad*. He may even have known these stories as they were already incorporated into epic poems. But we should not identify these epics with the texts of the *Aethiopis* or *Little Iliad* as fragmentarily known to us. We should not (in all probability) identify them with *any* texts. The formulaic style of the *Iliad* and *Odyssey* suggests they are somehow the product of a stage of oral transmission.[16] Homer himself will presumably have been acquainted with other orally transmitted epics and these may have included earlier versions of *Aethiopis* or *Little Iliad*. But the *Iliad* and *Odyssey* would appear to have been preserved in written texts earlier than the other poems of the Epic Cycle, which seem to have gradually assumed the status of sequels to or anticipations of the Homeric epics. By the time they took on the stable and permanent form of which we possess fragmentary knowledge, they would have been accurately termed 'post-Homeric'.

Authorship

Various traditions have come down to us from antiquity as to the authors of the poems in the Epic Cycle. Often the authorship is disputed (e.g. the *Cypria* is variously assigned to Homer, Stasinus or a certain Cyprias: see T 1-12 and below, p. 32). We have independent evidence as to the dates of some of these authors[17] and if this evidence were believed it would tell against the generally late dating of most of the cyclic epics advocated above (e.g. Arctinus, alleged author of the *Aethiopis* and *Sack of Troy*, is by some sources assigned a *floruit* of c.775 BC). However, there are numerous reasons why we should not accept this evidence.

For a start, it is now generally known that many of the impressively specific datings of early Greek poets preserved in later authors are totally unreliable and based on an arbitrary chronological 'chain' worked out in the second century BC. Thus even if there are good reasons to trust the attribution of individual epics to individual poets we would have no reliable independent information as to dates. But there are not even any good reasons.[18] Wilamowitz in the book cited below (p. 11, n.7) observed that our earliest and most reliable sources quoted the epics in question anonymously ('the author of the *Titanomachy*', 'the composer of the *Cypria*' etc.) or with considerable reservations about alleged authorship. Attributions come from late and unreliable sources. Then again, these sources often produce contradictory statements as to a poet's dating. And it is often easy to guess at least some of the reasons why an author is located in such and such a time (e.g. Eumelus and Arctinus assigned to the same Olympiad (see *Aethiopis* T 2) because both are credited with the composition of a *Titanomachy*; or Eugammon placed in 567 BC (*Telegony* T 2) because as a Cyrenean he must post-date Cyrene's founding (c.630 BC)).

We should not, then, place very much weight on these ancient traditions as to the chronology of the supposed cyclic poets. A relatively late individual may well have assigned epics hitherto anonymous or attributed to Homer to poets who happened to have nothing else to their names. The reasoning behind the attribution may have been relatively arbitrary and haphazard (e.g. the unusually entitled *Cypria* bestowed upon Stasinus because he was known to be from Cyprus). Such external evidence cannot outweigh the internal linguistic evidence of the fragments themselves which points inexorably to a late dating.[19]

Proclus and Apollodorus[20]

In the case of the poems within the Epic Cycle that deal with the Trojan War (i.e. all the epics from *Cypria* to *Telegony*) we happen to possess a source of information additional to the fragments mentioned above (p. 2). Proclus, an author of unknown date and origin, composed a *Chrestomathia* or *Summary of Useful Knowledge*. The later writer Photius (c.810-c.893 AD) in his *Bibliotheca* (or *Library*) gives us an outline of it, including some general remarks on the Epic Cycle (cf. p. 13 below on *Titanomachy* F 2). More importantly, Proclus' résumé of the Epic Cycle's Trojan poems is preserved in some MSS of Homer's *Iliad*: in other words, we are fortunate enough to possess extracts from the actual text of Proclus' prose summary of these poems.

Scholars have not proved invariably as grateful as we might have expected about this lucky addition to our knowledge of the Cycle's contents. Nineteenth-century German classical scholarship became progressively sceptical as a general principle (and often, particularly in the area of historical 'source-criticism', this scepticism was beneficial and appropriate). The fact that we do not know the precise identity of Proclus rather irrationally increased scepticism as to the reliability of his résumé. More reasonably, since some discrepancies were observed between his summary of the Trojan epics and actual fragments of them, suspicion naturally increased. Finally, at the end of the nineteenth century, an *Epitome* was published of the missing close to the *Bibliotheca* of Apollodorus, a mythological hand-book of about the first century BC. This epitome's summary of the stories relating to the Trojan War was soon perceived to be very close in wording and content to Proclus' alleged résumé of the Epic Cycle's Trojan epics. It was concluded that both derived from an earlier mythographic hand-book and that Proclus' claim to be summarising lost epics was finally and definitely exploded.

Such a conclusion in no way follows. The discrepancies between Proclus' summary and our actual fragmentary texts of the lost epics are easily explained when we consider what these summaries are doing in MSS of the *Iliad*. They have been transferred there to fulfill a new purpose: to remind the reader of the *Iliad* of episodes in the story of Troy so as to facilitate his understanding and enjoyment of Homer's epic. But the other Trojan epics from the Cycle, though their final form was influenced by a wish to fill details before and after the events of Homer's two poems, may have originally been independent compositions (p. 4), and in consequence sometimes disagreed with Homer's version of events (see e.g. below, pp. 40 and 47). These disagreements had to be removed (together with repetitions of events also present in *Iliad* and *Odyssey*) from Proclus' original summary when this was transformed into a preface to the *Iliad*: otherwise there would be unnecessary confusion.

Provided we bear this in mind, most of the discrepancies alluded to are explicable, and we may accept Proclus' résumé as a reliable source of evidence (though like all summaries it may sometimes omit material we would have liked to know). Apollodorus' *Epitome*, as we saw above, often echoes Proclus: in such cases we will conclude that it too is drawing (via who knows how many intermediate stages) on the relevant lost cyclic epic(s). Sometimes it will add details not in Proclus' résumé: these may often derive likewise from those epics and be valuable adjuncts to the information preserved in Proclus. But since Apollodorus is not avowedly and solely summarising lost epics, since he is only intermittently specific as to the identity of his sources, and since he can be shown elsewhere in his hand-book to switch from one source to the other without notice, we must be rather cautious in drawing upon the tradition enshrined in his work. In the chapters on the Trojan epics below (p. 32ff.) I occasionally mention those details in Apollodorus' *Epitome* which are likelier than not to derive from the Epic Cycle.

The value of the Epic Cycle

Let us finally return to the question we originally posed at the start of this Introduction: is the Epic Cycle, as recoverable by fragments and the (incomplete) summary of Proclus, worth studying today? We have already seen (above, p. 2) how Aristotle and the Alexandrian critics perceived that the poets of the Cycle were not only different from, but qualitatively inferior to, the poet of the *Iliad* and *Odyssey*. Aristotle's *Poetics* (1459b 1ff.) observes that, by comparison with Homer, both the *Cypria* and the *Little Iliad* lack unity (so that whereas only one or at the most two tragedies could be written exploiting the subject-matter of the Homeric poems, the episodic nature of the latter would supply plots for a large number of tragedies: cf. Athenaeus' remark about Sophocles cited above, p. 1). Modern scholars have developed this traditional contrast between Homer and the Epic Cycle along even more instructive lines.

As early as 1884, D.B. Monro[21] was pointing out that the Epic Cycle seems to have found room for all sorts of motifs and traditions that are strikingly absent from the *Iliad* and *Odyssey*. Shortly after the start of the twentieth century Andrew Lang[22] observed:

> Even in the few fragments of the so-called Cyclic poets...and in the sketches of the plots of the Cyclic poems which have reached us, there are survivals of barbaric customs – for example, of human sacrifice, and the belief in phantasms of the dead, even when the dead have been properly burned and buried – which do not appear in the *Iliad* and the *Odyssey*.... It is not easily conceivable that Homer was ignorant of any of these things...but he ignores them.

In 1918 Sir James Frazer, author of the famous study *The Golden Bough*, stated:[23]

> A comparison of early Hebrew traditions with their Babylonian counterparts enables us to appreciate how carefully the authors

or editors of Genesis have pruned away the grotesque and extravagant elements of legend and myth.... In their handiwork we can trace the same fine literary instinct which has similarly purified the Homeric poems from many gross and absurd superstitions, which, though they bear plain marks of an antiquity far greater than that of Homer, are known to us only through writings of much later ages.

In more recent times Jasper Griffin[24] has sensitively and thoroughly treated this aspect of the contrast between Homer and the Cyclic poets. It is indeed illuminating to discover just how selective is the heroic world depicted by the *Iliad* and – to a lesser extent – the *Odyssey*, and how it vigorously excludes elements of the fantastic, the grotesque, the excessively grim, or simply anything redolent of folk-tale or folk-superstition. It is also instructive to observe the poets of the Cycle shovelling this material back into their far less selective and less carefully considered poetic world. The narrative style of the cyclic epics also, as Griffin and others have seen, seems to have been vastly inferior to Homer's, judging from the few fragments of direct citation long enough to enable us to pass this verdict. In the following chapters on the individual epics I have consistently drawn attention to both classes of divergence.

All this, of course, while confirming and elaborating Homer's status as a great poet, might be thought to constitute good cause why the late twentieth century should *not* spend its time on the Epic Cycle as such. The plea that the Cycle's constituent poems must have had some merit to attract reworking by a Sophocles (see above, p. 1) or a Pindar (see below, p. 41) rings rather hollow: it is precisely the improvement of the second-rate by the first-rate that strikes the mind. The Epic Cycle is often claimed to have served as a source of inspiration for visual artists, especially vase-painters. This argument, also, needs to be treated cautiously, if for different reasons. Vase-painting often does seem to be attracted by mythical themes which also featured in the Epic Cycle, but the prospect that the former was directly inspired by the latter is far more difficult to prove than is generally realised,[25] especially since we possess intact none of the cyclic epics as such.

The main motive for continuing to study these poems must be what has already been stated as their main attraction in later antiquity (above,

p. 2). They did preserve, however inadequately and inelegantly, a good deal of interesting mythological information. In many cases they may have been the earliest literary sources to contain these details. Homer's elimination of the crudely fantastic allowed him to achieve a personal and inimitable poetic vision. But what Homer left out clearly appealed to a substantial number of Greeks – as witness the continued popularity of stories such as the all-too-vulnerable heel of Achilles, or Tydeus' savage gnawing of Melanippus' skull.[26] Homer's poetic world does not comprise the whole of the Hellenic outlook. The folk-tale motifs one finds preserved in the cyclic poets are often fascinating in their own right and widen our perspective, especially of the 'darker side' of Greek myth.

Notes

1. His source for this detail is Ion of Chios (*F.Gr.Hist.* 392 F 6), a contemporary of Sophocles: *Tr.G.F.* 4 T 75 Radt.
2. *Tr.G.F.* 4 T 136 Radt = *E.G.F.* *T 4.
3. In this section I am summarising the contents of my (cumbersomely titled) article 'Prolegomena and Paralegomena to a new edition (with commentary) of the Fragments of Early Greek Epic' published in the (equally cumbersomely titled) *Nachrichten der Akademie der Wissenschaften in Göttingen* 1 *phil.-hist. Kl.*2 (1986) 91ff. (hereafter *NGG*).
4. Cf. scholia on *Od.* 16.195 and 17.25; Aristoxenus fr. 91(1) Wehrli = *Vit. Hom. et Hes.* p. 32, 20 Wilamowitz.
5. On Proclus' late prose summary of the plots of the Trojan epics, see p. 6.
6. The concept of linguistically 'late' features that can be used for a relative dating of portions within the *Iliad* and *Odyssey*, and of Hesiod and the *Homeric Hymns* relative to Homer, is a familiar one, though the definition of 'late' needs to be handled with caution (see, for instance, R. Janko, *Homer, Hesiod and the Hymns* (Cambridge 1982), General Index sv. 'innovation, linguistic').
7. *Homerische Untersuchungen* p. 366.
8. *Sprachliche Untersuchungen zu Homer* (1916) p. 178ff., esp. 181ff.
9. Since the *Cypria* and the *Little Iliad* are represented by a relatively large number of directly quoted fragments and the *Thebais* and *Sack of Troy* by a relatively small number, the negative evidence for earlier dating of the latter pair is not very strong. See my remarks in *Glotta* (1989).
10. For instance, J. Griffin, *JHS* 97 (1977) p. 39, n.9, after referring to Wackernagel's treatment, follows another scholar in placing 'the composition of the Cyclic epics in general in the late seventh century'.
11. The naïve schematism that underlies this approach is still unexpectedly influential: for a vigorous attack upon it, see R.L. Fowler, *The Nature of Early Greek Lyric: Three Preliminary Studies* (Toronto 1987) p. 3ff.
12. M.L. West, *The Hesiodic Catalogue of Women* (Oxford 1985) p. 130ff. See also J.R. March, *The Creative Poet* (*BICS* Suppl. 49 (1987)) p. 157ff. (preferring a date of c.580-70).

13. Cf. A. Severyns, *Le Cycle Epique dans l'École d'Aristarque* (Paris 1928).
14. Cf. *NGG* 2 (1986) 109f.
15. Wolfgang Kullmann, *Die Quellen der Ilias* (Hermes Einzelschriften 14 (1960)). The review by D.L. Page, *CR* 11 (1961) 205ff. exposed most of the weaknesses in the book referred to here and others beside.
16. In fairness to Kullmann it should be added that his subsequent articles on this and related topics reveal progressively increasing awareness of weaknesses in his book and a progressively increasing readiness to correct and replace them with the more flexible and sophisticated approach here outlined.
17. But not all of them. Thus when the *Oxford Classical Dictionary*^{2} (1970) sv. 'Stasinus of Cyprus' anonymously assigned the hypothetical date '?8th c(entury) BC' to this poet, it was relying on nothing more specific than an untrustworthy biographical anecdote (below, p. 32) and an unprovable feeling that the *Cypria* he is supposed to have composed must be very early.
18. Cf. *NGG* 2 (1986) 99f.
19. For completeness' sake I preface each chapter below with a brief account of the various authors to whom the Cycle's epics were assigned in antiquity. But little faith should be placed in these attributions.
20. Cf. *NGG* 2 (1986) 100ff.
21. *JHS* 5 (1884) 1ff.
22. *Anthropology and the Classics* (Oxford 1908) p. 44f.
23. *Folk-Lore in the Old Testament* 2.394.
24. 'The Epic Cycle and the uniqueness of Homer', *JHS* 97 (1977) 39ff. There are also some suggestive remarks by Sir John Forsdyke in Chapter 6 ('Cyclic Characters': p. 110ff.) of his book *Greece before Homer: Ancient Chronology and Mythology* (London 1956) which includes some material not mentioned by Griffin.
25. See the remarks of R.M. Cook in *BABESCH* (*Annual Papers on Classical Archaeology*) 58 (1983) 1ff.
26. The former possibly featured in the *Aethiopis* (see p. 55f.); the latter certainly featured in the *Thebais* (p. 26f.), and may fairly be said to have haunted the European consciousness ever since, as witness Statius' *Thebaid* 8.740ff., Dante's presentation of Count Ugolino in Cantos 32-3 of the Divine Comedy's *Inferno* or Delacroix's painting of Dante and Vergil crossing the Styx (now in the Louvre), to cite a mere handful of instances that echo the scene.

2: The Titanomachy

The first poem within the Epic Cycle was the *Titanomachy*, variously attributed to Eumelus of Corinth (T 2, F 3, F 5, 8) and to Arctinus (F 5), also allegedly author of the *Aethiopis* (below, p. 51) and the *Sack of Troy* (p. 71). It is often asserted that this poem will, in fact, have been (for completeness' sake) preceded in the Cycle by a *Theogony*, and that the contents of this lost *Theogony* can be recovered from an inspection of the opening portion of Apollodorus' *Library*. For Apollodorus (it is argued) drew on this 'Cyclic *Theogony*', and his summary reveals it to have been Orphic in character and content. I believe that we should be very sceptical about this theory and that Apollodorus' opening section is actually indebted to Hesiod's *Theogony*, the apparent differences and disagreements between the two being explicable on the assumption that the mythographer has reworked his source and changed it by the processes of omission, rearrangement, and simplification.

F 2 (from Photius' recapitulation of Proclus' summary (see above, p. 6)) states that the Epic Cycle opened with the coupling of Gê (Mother Earth) and Uranus (Heaven) and those who believe in an (unattested) 'Cyclic *Theogony*' refer this quintessentially theogonic detail to its contents. But we know from F1 that the Cycle's *Titanomachy* contained the information that Uranus (Heaven) was the son of Aether (Sky). In other words, just as Hesiod's *Theogony* included a Titanomachy (at lines 617ff.), so the Cycle's *Titanomachy* seems to have included a Theogony, or details relevant thereto, near its beginning.

What is (or was) a Titanomachy? It is the battle whereby Cronus and his brothers, the Titans, were defeated and ousted from their position as rulers of the Universe by Zeus and his brothers and offspring. The older powers succumb to the Olympians, who represent the next generation of gods. Strictly speaking, the Titanomachy should be clearly distinguished from the Gigantomachy, which represents an occasion later in time when the Olympians, now the firmly established controllers of the cosmos, find their own power threatened by a motley crew of giants and monsters inclined to dispute their authority and quelled only with difficulty and the participation of Heracles on the Olympians' side. The two events are different in other ways too (for instance, the Gigantomachy is a very popular subject in art, while the Titanomachy features there little, if at all). But it would be absurd for us to be too severe about this, since the Greeks themselves, from as early as Euripides onwards, confused (or did not strive too officiously to keep distinct) one with the other, and the coalescence is endemic in Roman writers. Sometimes Gigantomachy may have been written for Titanomachy (or *vice versa*) by mistake, since the words look very similar in Greek script (this has happened in the source that supplies us with F 9 of the *Titanomachy*).

To return to F 1, we may begin by observing that its apparent use of a family-tree to explain the origin of the universe is a common ploy in Theogonies, Hesiodic and other. Our fragment's statement that Uranus (Heaven) was the son of Aether (Sky) may be explicable in terms of another fragment, this time belonging to the Greek lyric poet Alcman (seventh century BC). According to him (fr.61P) Uranus was the son of Akmôn (a similar tradition appears to be implied by Antimachus fr.44 W and Callimachus fr.498 Pf). The Greek word *akmôn* means not only 'anvil' but also perhaps 'meteoric stone'; and early Greek literature shows vestiges of a primitive belief that the sky was actually made out of stone, which would neatly elucidate our fragment. The role it attributes to Aether is without precise parallel but has approximate analogies in the cosmogonies of some early Greek poets (e.g. Musaeus 2B14 DK, Acusilaus 9B1 DK).

F 2 we have already considered above (p. 13). F 3 relates to a group of fabulous brothers known as 'the Hundred-Handers', who are named, for instance, in Hes. *Th.* 149: Cottus, Briareus and Gyges. Homer (in *Il.* 1.403f) tells us (exploiting a wide-spread and familiar folk-tale motif) that Briareus is the gods' name for the being whom mortals call Aegaeon, and Aegaeon would seem to be the name under which the monster passed in the *Titanomachy*. This poem depicted him as the offspring of Gê (Earth) and Pontus (Sea), in contrast to Hesiod, who made the three brothers offspring of Gê and Uranus (*Th.* 147). Why our epic thus differed in the question of the father of Aegaeon/Briareus it is not easy to say.

We may, however, observe that in the Iliadic episode alluded to above, the sea-goddess Thetis fetches him to Olympus, which may conceivably entail that Homer located him in the sea, as does our fragment. Note also that Greek literature and belief often portrays monsters of this sort as the offspring of marine deities (cf. Hes. *Th.* 270ff. etc.). Whatever the relevance of such obervations, it must be stressed that our fragment is at variance both with Hes. *Th.* 639ff. and the Iliadic episode: for these passages explicitly or implicitly present this monster as an ally of the Olympians, whereas F 2 says he fought on the side of the Titans. A similar state of affairs seems to be implied at Vergil *Aen.* 10.565ff. with its picture of Aegaeon opposed to Jupiter. We must again confess our ignorance as to the motive behind this divergence.

In contrast with Aegaeon, who features in Homer, F 4 sets before us a group of motifs which seem to be sedulously avoided by him: the familiar folk-tale motif of the Sun's chariot and the four horses that draw it. It appears that our epic supplied the names of the creatures: Eous (meaning 'of the dawn') and Aethops ('the bright one'); Bronte ('thunder') and Sterope ('lightning'). The first two names have a significance too obvious to require explanation. The last two remind us of the names of those two Cyclopes who produce (respectively) thunder and lightning, as given by (among others) Hes. *Th.* 140: Brontes and Steropes. The belief that a god's (or the gods') horses have literally thundering hooves is widespread and obviously underlies our passage. Whether F 4's context was merely that everyday event, the Sun's passage across the heavens, or whether (as in some late sources) the Sun god Helios was specifically mentioned as participating in (or markedly refraining from) the battle between the Olympians and the Titans we have no way of knowing.

F 5 preserves a single hexameter from the *Titanomachy*:

And in their midst danced the father of men and gods.

In its different way this fragment too is as unHomeric as F 4. Homer's Zeus may not be consistently dignified but it is hard to conceive him as dancing. Indeed no god dances in Homer. Apollo does, in the *Homeric Hymn* named after him (v.189ff., 514ff.), but as the god of song and dance he surely constitutes a special case. Pindar (fr.148 Sn.) has a more general vision of dancing gods but Zeus is still not specifically named. The god's dance is a primeval Indo-European motif but most scholars have felt that the *Titanomachy's* detail of Zeus dancing requires some special explanation and have generally located this in the divine rejoicing that will have followed the successful conclusion of the Olympians' war against the Titans (a number of passages by later authors (e.g. Tibull. 2.5.9f. and Sen. *Ag.* 339ff.) have been interpreted as reflecting some such tradition of rejoicing). Zeus will have been celebrating the first day of his rule, and as such the act will have been very special, indeed never-to-be-repeated. A partial analogy cited by some from the Old Testament, would be 2 Samuel 6:14 where, after the capture of Jerusalem, 'David danced before the Lord with all his might'.

F 6 deals with Chiron, a particularly humane and wise centaur (see below, p. 17) whose beneficent attitude to mankind is often praised in Greek literature (e.g. Pind. *Pyth.* 3.1ff. and Eur. *I.A.* 710). The two verses in question clearly emanate from a longer list of kindnesses towards mortals:

> And he brought the race of mortals to a state of justice by revealing to them the use of binding oaths and joyous feasts and the signs of heaven.

In other words the *Titanomachy* treated Chiron as a type of 'culture-hero' comparable with Prometheus (see, for instance, *Prometheus Bound* v.447ff.) or Palamedes (see below, p. 48). Such 'culture-heroes' are conspicuously absent from Homer; and, though Chiron is mentioned a handful of times in the *Iliad*, that poem keeps quiet about the tradition that he acted as tutor to such heroes as Achilles or his father Peleus (see below, p. 50). A poem attributed to Hesiod in antiquity and known as *Cheirônos Hypothêkai* (*Chiron's Wise Saws*) reflects the same view of the noble beast (for reference to and fragments of it see Merkelbach and West's *Fragmenta Hesiodea* p. 143ff.).

F 7 mentions the gold cup of the Sun which was nightly used to transport the Sun god over the sea from his setting in the West back to his palace in the East. Like the Sun's chariot (in F 4 above) this is a popular motif (with parallels the world over) which numerous later writers mention but which Homer omits from his picture of the world.

F 8 is a fascinating but baffling fragment of two lines' compass:

And on (*or* in) it the golden-faced scaly swimming fish sport as they move through the immortal water

— delightfully decorative lines, but not easily fitted into any plausible context within a *Titanomachy*. Largely because of the striking reference to 'golden-faced...fish', scholars have contemplated assigning the passage to an *ecphrasis* or formal description of the contents of a work of art. One such description, from an *ecphrasis* which gives the poem to which it belongs its title (*The Shield of Heracles*, attributed in antiquity to Hesiod), does indeed contain a superficially similar episode. At lines 207ff. we find an account of a harbour depicted on Heracles' shield: 'silver dolphins' are shown, and also 'bronze fish'. Could the 'it' on or in which our fragment's fish appear be a similar artefact? An objection is that in the Hesiodic *Shield*, as in all other instances of the *ecphrasis*, from the Homeric Shield of Achilles (*Il.* 18.483ff.) down to the description in Ap. Rhod. 1.730ff., the verbs employed are regularly in the past tense (early Greek poetry does not employ the historic present). Unless one emends our fragment's present tense to past (which can be done) the hypothesis of an *ecphrasis* may not hold. In any case, the fragment's word for 'golden-faced' (*chrysôpis*) is also the name of a perfectly normal fish (the Mediterranean 'Gilthead' or Dorade).

F 9 explains how Chiron came to be a centaur – half-man, half-horse. His father Cronus changed himself into a horse and mated with Philyra daughter of Oceanus. This story recurs in, for instance, Pherecydes *F.Gr.Hist.* 3 F 50 and Ap. Rhod. 2.1232ff. The Epic Cycle was by no means averse to such tales (as witness Zeus' metamorphosis into a goose at *Cypria* F 8: see below, p. 38). Homer characteristically has no time for shape-changing deities and it is no coincidence that when Zeus lists his various mortal amours at *Il.* 14.315ff., though Europe and Danae are among them, nothing is said of his metamorphosis into bull or golden shower.

F 10 refers to the Hesperides, nymphs who guard a tree that bears golden apples in the remote west. The text that preserves this fragment is incomplete and its tenor is not quite certain. Perhaps it originally stated that in the *Titanomachy* the guardian(s) of the apples were in fact represented neither as Hesperides nor (according to some other authors, e.g. Acusilaus 9B5 DK) as winged monsters called Harpies, but as the snake referred to by, for instance, Hes. *Th.* 333ff. It is a traditional folk-tale motif that a serpent makes a suitable protector of treasures of various sorts. Not surprisingly, therefore, Homer has nothing to say of the Hesperides or their treasure.

3: The Oedipodeia

The story and sufferings of Oedipus were a popular subject in Attic tragedy. It would be interesting to know which of the details in, for instance, Sophocles' *Oedipus Tyrannus* were the playwright's own invention and which inherited. And it would be interesting to know which of the inherited features were to be found in earlier epic and the Cycle's *Oedipodeia* in particular. Interesting but impossible. We only possess two fragments of the *Oedipodeia*, together with part of an inscription that informs us that the epic was composed by a certain Cinaethon and was 6,600 lines long.

Oedipus' legend is made up of a number of folk-tale motifs that can be paralleled the world over. For instance: the oracle that warns a man (in this case Laius) not to beget a son. The exposed infant (in this case Oedipus). The baffling riddle (in this case posed by the Sphinx). The hero who solves the riddle and wins the princess' hand. F 1 quotes two hexameters from the *Oedipodeia* which concern the Sphinx's activity before Oedipus arrived on the scene: Haemon son of Creon seems to have been specified as one of the Sphinx's victims:

> But by far the fairest and most desirable of all, the dear son of blameless Creon, noble Haemon, <the Sphinx destroyed>.

This tradition of Haemon's death recurs in later authors: for instance, Apollod. 3.5.8 where the sad event spurs Creon into proclaiming that whosoever solves the Sphinx's riddle shall receive the kingship of Thebes (left vacant by Laius' death) and shall marry Laius' widow. Perhaps this was the context of Haemon's death in the *Oedipodeia*. Vase-paintings often depict the Sphinx carrying off a youthful male victim. The language used of Haemon in our fragment is surprisingly erotic for epic and we are reminded that in Attic tragedy (in particular Sophocles' *Antigone*) Haemon is represented as surviving to become the fiancé of Antigone.

Several late authors preserve in different form five or so hexameters purporting to be the Sphinx's riddle. The *Oedipodeia* doubtless quoted the riddle, but the relationship between that and the verses preserved by the late authors in question is quite uncertain.

Oedipus solved the Sphinx's riddle and married Laius' widow, oblivious that she was also his own mother. F 2 of our epic (from Pausanias 9.5.10) deals with what it had to say about this marriage and its offspring. Since Pausanias refers to the *Oedipodeia* after quoting *Od.* 11.271ff., it will be best if we first clear our minds as to the extant epic and then move on to the lost poem. During the *Nekyia* Odysseus reports himself as having seen in the Underworld Oedipus' mother (whom he calls Epicaste, unlike the Attic tragedians who know her as Jocasta). Her marriage to her own son is mentioned and then the passage proceeds with the statement that the gods *at once* made things known to mankind. Epicaste committed suicide but Oedipus went on ruling in Thebes in accordance with the gods' baleful designs.

Not unreasonably, Pausanias infers from the Greek word for 'at once' that the Homeric passage envisages no children of this incestuous marriage. This contrasts with the two pairs of brothers and sisters (Polyneices and Eteocles; Antigone and Ismene) familiar from the Attic tragedians. In Sophocles' *Oedipus Tyrannus*, for instance, the revelation of Oedipus' crime is postponed long enough for all four offspring to be relatively grown-up. The most convincing explanation of this detail cites Homer's reluctance to handle excessively grim stories of family conflict and retribution (compare his treatment of the house of Atreus: see below, p. 44f.). So here, though he cannot omit the central issue of incest, he says nothing of Oedipus' self-blinding (so vividly portrayed in tragedy) and will not have any children born of the incestuous union (compare his refusal to grant offspring to the analogously improper liaison of Helen and Paris: below, p. 39f.).

Pausanias adopts a different explanation and argues that the four children familiar from Attic drama were begotten by Oedipus not upon his mother but on a totally different woman called Euryganeia. And he says this is the version followed in the *Oedipodeia*. Most scholars take him at his word and conjure up an earlier 'epic' version of the Oedipus story very different from the harrowing account known from the tragedians.

In this alleged epic version, Oedipus takes his sufferings a good deal more calmly, does not blind himself, continues to rule in Thebes, marries again and becomes the father of four children, and finally dies and is buried in Thebes (this last detail is inferred from *Il.* 23.678ff. and Hes. fr. 192 MW). This version is so astonishingly at odds with the cataclysmic tone of Attic tragedy's handling of the theme that we should pause and ask ourselves whether this is really the only conclusion to be drawn from Pausanias' words.

The answer is 'No'. In the nineteenth century, when German classical scholars were instinctively sceptical about a great many statements in ancient authors in general and Pausanias in particular, a different explanation was put forward. Pausanias has made a mistake: Oedipus' wife and mother was called Euryganeia in the *Oedipodeia*, just as she was called Epicaste in the *Odyssey*, Jocasta in Greek tragedy, Eurycleia in Epimenides 3 B 15 DK and Astymedusa in a scholion on *Il.* 4.376. She was the only woman who bore children to Oedipus, and those children were, as one might expect, Polyneices, Eteocles, Antigone and Ismene. This, after all, is the version reported in Apollod. 3.5.8. It is true that some authors do report a version that Oedipus remarried and had the four above-mentioned children by his second wife (Pisander *F.Gr.Hist.* 16 F 10 and Pherecydes *F.Gr.Hist.* 3 F 95) but these may represent late attempts to reduce the horror inherent in the story by having the children born of a perfectly normal union just as Homer seeks in a different way to eliminate the ghastly aspects of the tale.

At the very least, this hypothesis, that Pausanias is mistaken in inferring that Euryganeia was not merely a different name for, but also a different person from, Oedipus' mother, deserves to be treated as an hypothesis no less plausible than the traditional explanation which has such drastic implications for the early literary treatments of the Oedipus myth. Indeed it is salutary to be reminded just how little we know of this legend before the time of the Attic tragedians. That ignorance certainly extends to most other portions of the *Oedipodeia*: we do not have the slightest idea of how far in time its narrative extended, for instance, whether there were any overlaps with the subject-matter of the *Thebais*, or whether it aimed at filling in the background to that epic.

4: The Thebais

Of all attributions to Homer of epics over and above the *Iliad* and *Odyssey*, that involving the *Thebais* has the most venerable credentials. Pausanias 9.9.1ff. (= *Thebais* T 1) tells us that the seventh century elegiac poet Callinus assigned it to Homer; adds the Greek equivalent of 'many distinguished scholars accept this attribution'; and rounds off for good measure with the statement that he himself puts it next to *Iliad* and *Odyssey* in merit. 'Many distinguished scholars' of today have been perhaps too impressed by all this. We should surely be cautious in accepting the valuation of a now lost epic by an author of the second century AD, and Callinus may merely have credited to Homer one or two words or phrases which a later writer recognised in the text of the *Thebais* (for a similar problem involving Pindar and the *Cypria*, see below, p. 32).

Homer's *Iliad* contains a number of allusions to the earlier expedition of the Seven against Thebes. Many of these references are paradigmatic or exemplary: that is they are variously addressed by various characters to Diomedes son of Tydeus, and cite various deeds of valour performed by the illustrious father in connection with the Theban war in order to encourage the son to emulation or to contrast him unfavourably with his greater father. Though these passages have Tydeus very much at their centre (for the reason just given), they clearly presuppose a wider background of the war against Thebes. So nineteenth-century scholars spent much time pondering whether Homer's 'source' for these references might be the *Thebais* of which we now possess a mere handful of fragments. The twentieth century had a greater awareness of the complexities inherent in the concept of oral tradition and its relevance to Homer (see above, p. 4f.). The notion of 'sources' no longer seems as appropriate for a poetic composition as for a historical work, and the possibility that Homer himself might invent (for paradigmatic purposes) mythological details such as those found in the Iliadic mentions of

Tydeus is now taken very seriously. Nevertheless, Homer will, of course, have been acquainted with any number of traditions about the war against Thebes which features as a typical subject for heroic poetry from the time of Hesiod's *Works and Days* (v.162) onwards. Some of these traditions may, by Homer's time, have already been enshrined in epics and one of these epics may have been the forefather (so to speak) of the cyclic *Thebais* (compare the remarks above, p. 2ff., on the likely date of the Cyclic epics).

We happen to possess the very first line of the *Thebais* (F 1):

> Of Argos sing, goddess, the thirsty city from which the lords
> <of the expedition against Thebes set forth...>

The injunction to a goddess (i.e. a Muse) is the same as in the *Iliad*'s opening verse (indeed the Greek words for 'sing' and 'goddess' are identical and in an identical position as second and third words within the hexameter). But whereas the opening words of the *Iliad* ('anger') and the *Odyssey* ('the man') handily encapsulate one of the central themes of each epic, the *Thebais* surprisingly opened with a mention not of the city which is to be attacked (as the *Little Iliad* (see below, p. 60) started with the word 'Ilium') but with the city *from which* the attack was mustered. One is not, however, to infer that Argos was a particular object of the poem's interests or sympathies (see below, p. 25ff.). Our quoted verse breaks off danglingly with the words 'from which the lords', but it is easy to infer some such immediate continuation as supplied above. The way in which the opening noun is later picked up by a relative clause is idiomatic for an epic proem: compare the *Iliad* ('The Anger...which'), *Odyssey* ('The man...who'), and see below, p. 61, on the first two lines of the *Little Iliad*.

The *Thebais* seems to have explained how the expedition of the Seven against Thebes came into being by referring to the famous curse which Oedipus invoked against his sons Polyneices and Eteocles. The two longest fragments from our epic provided motivations for this curse in two different (but not incompatible) ways: F 2:

> But the godly hero, yellow-haired Polyneices, first of all set
> before Oedipus the fair table, made out of silver, which had

belonged to Cadmus. But next he filled the golden fair goblet full of sweet wine. But Oedipus when he perceived that there had been set before him his own father <Laius'> honoured possessions, a great evil fell upon his heart and straightaway he invoked baleful curses upon his own sons, both of them (and this did not go unnoticed by the Erinys of the gods), to the effect that they would not † divide their patrimony on friendly terms, † but rather would ever have wars and battles between them both...

Later writers (especially the Attic tragedians) provided different explanations for the grounds, terms and context of the old man's curse. In the second fragment of the *Thebais* it seems that Oedipus' anger was roused by the unthinking way in which Polyneices (treated as the wicked and impious brother by most later writers) set before him objects which reminded him of his former prosperity and of the father whom he had unintentionally supplanted and killed. (Athenaeus, who quotes the fragment, adds that Oedipus had specifically forbidden the goblet to be brought before him.) Polyneices alone is mentioned as offender (perhaps our epic, like many later authors, regarded him as the elder brother) but both brothers are cursed. The Greek verb which tells us that Oedipus 'perceived' the slight is no evidence for whether this epic depicted him as self-blinded or not. Scholars have expressed their disappointment at this passage as literature: the curse should have functioned as a hair-raising climax of horror (as its equivalent does in Sophocles *O.C.* 1370ff.). Instead it is despatched in the matter-of-fact style characteristic of much of the Cycle, with clumsy repetition (a 'fair' table and a 'fair' wine-goblet; the Greek for 'but' is used three times in five lines).

F 3 mentions a different curse on a different occasion:

When <Oedipus> noticed the haunch he cast it upon the ground and uttered a speech: 'Woe is me! My sons have sent this to me as a great insult'. And he prayed to Zeus the king and the other immortals that <the sons> should descend to the house of Hades slain at each other's hands.

On this occasion it would seem Oedipus was expecting a more honourable portion of the sacrificed animal and was angered on receiving a (to him) relatively dishonourable part. Again the Greek verb for 'noticed' implies nothing as to his blindness or lack of it. (An anonymous fragment of tragedy, quoted by the scholion which is our source for *Thebais* F 3, refers to Oedipus as *handling* the offending portion (*Tr.G.F.* 2 F 458.6f. Snell-Kannicht): perhaps this is below epic dignity.) F 3 is textually corrupt but even so it is another disappointing treatment of the curse-motif. The terse one-line speech by Oedipus is typical of the Cycle's cursory handling of *oratio recta*, one of the great glories of the Homeric poems, and an effective means of characterisation in the *Iliad* and *Odyssey*. Here, by contrast, the result is paltry. Nevertheless, it looks as if, especially in view of the allusions to mutual slaughter, this curse was meant to be consequent to and more of a climax than that embodied in F 2.

Later authors give different accounts of how Oedipus' curse began to take effect on the brothers after his death. The most straightforward account has Eteocles expel Polyneices by force and thus seize power in Thebes. Other writers picture Polyneices as voluntarily departing from the city as part of an arrangement where (in a futile attempt to avoid the curse's fulfilment) the brothers would reign over Thebes in alternate years. Whatever the precise details, Polyneices traditionally arrives at the court of Adrastus in Argos, marries that king's daughter and persuades him to lend him his approval (and forces) for an assault upon Thebes.

Authors give similarly differing lists of the famous 'Seven against Thebes' who constituted the leaders of this assault. The oldest account we have extant is in Aeschylus' play of that name (375ff.) where they are listed as Tydeus, Capaneus, Eteoclus, Hippomedon, Parthenopaeus, Amphiaraus and Polyneices. Aeschylus' tragedy is of the surviving sources closest in time to our epic, and the *Thebais*' roll-call was probably much the same. In Aeschylus' tragedy and in the Attic tragedians generally, the seven chieftains are invariably presented as frightening specimens of pride, brutality and hybris. So persistent and deep-rooted is this tradition that scholars have generally concluded that they were thus presented in some early and influential epic, to wit the *Thebais*. If so, we will have indirect evidence for another interesting comparison between Homer and the Epic Cycle since the *Iliad's* complex sympathy for *both* Greeks *and* Trojans is well-known. The *Thebais*, by contrast, seems to have portrayed the invaders from Argos as semi-monsters (with the exception of Amphiaraus: see below, p. 27f.). Tydeus and Capaneus are traditionally the worst. (F 8 contains detail as to how Tydeus' father Oeneus won Tydeus' mother Periboea as a prize in the spoil following upon the sack of a city.) Capaneus is regularly portrayed, in art and literature, as the archetypal instance of hybris, struck down by Zeus' thunderbolt as he boastfully scales the Theban battlements. If (as most scholars surmise) this detail derives from the *Thebais*, we have a further contrast with Homer, in whose more urbane epic world Zeus nowhere intervenes so crudely and directly (nor do heroes so behave as to invite such drastic punishment). The Cyclic epics were different: a parallel to what is here inferred for the *Thebais* occurs in the destruction of the impious Ajax at Athena's hands in the *Returns Home* (below, p. 78f.).

Several direct fragments have survived which specify the names and fates of some of the seven chieftains. F 4 contains the not very exciting piece of information that the warrior who killed Parthenopaeus was called Periclymenus. F 5 on the death of Tydeus is more interesting: Tydeus was wounded by Melanippus who in turn was killed by Amphiaraus. Amphiaraus then (for reasons we shall consider below, p. 28) brought Melanippus' head to the dying Tydeus who vented his anger by gnawing at its brain. This repulsive act so appalled Athena that she turned away in disgust though she had intended to bring him immortality. Tydeus, realising this, begged that she at least bestow it on his son. Athena's special patronage recalls several episodes in the *Iliad* where exemplary references to Tydeus presuppose a similar relationship (see above, p. 22) but in all other respects the episode is intensely unHomeric: no such grisly act of cannibalism is allowable in the *Iliad*, least of all in connection with Tydeus, allusions to whom are uniformly favourable. Then again, for Homer the gap between mortals and immortals is crucial and unbridgeable, a source of much of the *Iliad*'s tragedy and pathos. Not even Zeus can bestow immortality upon a friend or favourite (cf. *Il.* 16.431ff.) with the ease obviously presupposed in the *Thebais*. Later accounts would suggest that the immortality envisaged took the form of a drug or potion, a common folk-tale motif stretching back to the Ancient Near East. Successful immortalisation of Diomedes seems implied by our fragment, and such a tradition is represented by Ibycus fr. 294 P and

Pindar *Nemean* 10.7.

F 6 deals with the flight from the battlefield of the defeated leader of the seven, Adrastus:

> wearing begrimed clothes and riding on Arion the dark-maned horse.

He alone of the seven survived to reach home. It seems that the poet of the *Thebais* supplied some parenthetic detail about the parentage of Arion who was the offspring of Poseidon and an Erinys or Fury. Poseidon had metamorphosed himself into a horse and coupled with the Erinys in equine shape. The horse thus begotten was born and handed from Poseidon to the mortal Copreus and reached Adrastus via Heracles. The passage of a gift or possession from the gods through various mortal hands to its present owner is a frequent motif in epic (compare, for instance, the description of Agamemnon's sceptre in *Il.* 2.100ff.) but again the fragment has a markedly unHomeric ring with its picture of divine shape-changing. The most obvious parallel is Chiron's metamorphosis in F 7 of the *Titanomachy* (see above, p. 16), but other Cyclic analogies could be cited (see below, p. 37f.).

F 7 implies that when Pindar (*Ol.* 6.15ff.) represents Adrastus as mourning the loss of Amphiaraus, skilled both as seer and warrior, he is somehow indebted to the *Thebais*. A tradition mentioned explicitly only by later writers depicts Amphiaraus as able to foresee his own death should he participate in the Theban war. He therefore hid himself at home until Polyneices bribed his wife Eriphyle to reveal his whereabouts. As he set off for certain destruction Amphiaraus sternly enjoined his eldest son Alcmaeon to avenge him by killing his mother when he reached maturity. This 'Setting out of Amphiaraus' became a popular scene in vase-painting. Some late sources mention a literary 'Setting out of Amphiaraus' in a way which does not make it clear whether they are referring to a separate epic with this title or (as is more likely) an episode within the *Thebais* itself (F 9). For this episode to have featured as significantly as seems to have been the case, the preceding sequence of hiding and exposure must have also featured. The unHomeric picture of a cowardly reluctance to go to war is best paralleled by the similar skulking of Odysseus in the *Cypria* (see below, p. 42). Apollod. 3.6.8

tells us that Amphiaraus hated Tydeus for having persuaded the Argives into the attack on Thebes which he knew would cause his own death. Knowing also, by the same magic powers, that Athena intended to make Tydeus immortal, he betrayed the latter into the disgusting act of retribution (above, p. 26) which alienated the goddess. It is highly likely that this motivation derives from the *Thebais*. After the defeat of the Theban assault, Amphiaraus fled the field and was swallowed up, together with his chariot and horses, by the earth. So say later sources, and they are surely echoing the lost *Thebais*. Amphiaraus' end is appropriate: Greek popular belief often located seers beneath the earth.

5: The Epigoni

Familiarity with the story of the Seven's assault on Thebes may have dulled our awareness of just how unusual the framework of the tale is. Unlike most other accounts of the siege of a city, in particular that of the Trojan War, it deals with failure not success: the Seven's onslaught is frustrated, their army defeated, all the leaders bar one destroyed.

It is hardly surprising, therefore, that the notion of a second, successful and avenging expedition against Thebes arose at some time. This expedition is already presupposed at *Il.* 4.403ff. Symmetry entailed that the leaders of this expedition be the offspring of those chieftains engaged in the earlier unsuccessful attempt: Diomedes son of Tydeus, Alcmaeon son of Amphiaraus and so on.

The epic known as the *Epigoni* was therefore, in all likelihood, conceived as a deliberate continuation of the existing *Thebais* (several analogies for epic poems of this sort could be cited). It too was at one period assigned to Homer, though our knowledge of this attribution stems from authors (especially Herodotus 4.32 = T 1) who themselves cast doubt on its plausibility (compare Herodotus' remarks on the authorship of the *Cypria* (below, p. 32)).

We happen to possess the epic's opening line (F 1):

> Now again let us begin, Muses, the tale of younger men.

The younger men are, of course, the Epigoni, the sons of the leaders of the abortive campaign. The plurality of Muses, as opposed to the singular goddess invoked at the openings of the *Iliad*, *Odyssey*, and *Thebais* (see above, p. 23), is not at all significant or striking: early Greek poets refer interchangeably in such contexts to Muse or Muses without intending any particular point. Such poets likewise regularly use the Greek word for 'now' when passing to a new subject, even at the start of a poem. And the word 'again' is often used in invocations to the

Muse(s), implying 'inspire me again, as you have so often done in the past'. It need not here allude to a preceding poem (the *Thebais*) to which the *Epigoni* is proclaiming itself sequel. We cannot be sure whether 'let us begin' is an instance of plural for singular (the poet referring to himself), or whether it is a genuine plural including the poet *and* the Muses, a sort of combination of the invocation to the Muse of the *Iliad, Odyssey* and *Thebais* (F 1) with the 'I sing' formula of the *Little Iliad* (F 1). There is no shortage of parallels for the latter hypothesis with its implicit picture of Muse(s) and poet collaborating over a song.

As we saw with the first fragment of the *Thebais* (above, p. 23), it is idiomatic for an epic to state its theme initially and then elaborate the statement through a pendant relative clause ('The anger...which', 'The man...who'). It has therefore been suggested that the second verse of the *Epigoni* will have contained a like relative ('The younger men...<who succeeded in capturing Thebes>' *vel sim*.).

We have regrettably few other fragments of the *Epigoni* and they do not touch on themes which will have been central to the poem. F 2 tells us that the Hyperboreans, a legendary race living, as their name suggests, to the far North, were mentioned in our poem, in what context we cannot guess. F 3 presents a detail about Manto the daughter of Tiresias (see below, p. 78) who went to Delphi, married Rhacius of Mycenae, then repaired to Colophon where she lamented the sack of her native city and received the name Clarus because of her tears. The story exploited a familiar folk-tale motif, for Manto was instructed to marry whomever she encountered <coming out of the Delphic temple>. The whole episode is actually assigned by its source to the *Thebais*, but it begins with the statement that Manto was sent to Delphi by the Epigoni, so the attribution is likely to be a slip.

It is often assumed that the famous story of the Teumesian fox (an uncatchable creature) and Celphalus' hound (which nothing could escape) featured in the *Epigoni* (*Fr. incert. loc. intra Cycl.* 1): in fact its source assigns it to the authors of *ta Thêbaika* (Theban stories) and says it comes from the Epic Cycle. So *Thebais* (or even perhaps *Oedipodeia*) are equally plausible resting-places. The actual story was that when the inescapable met the uncatchable Zeus had to resolve the dilemma by changing both to stone: whatever the exact epic involved, the episode clearly exemplifies the Cycle's love of the magical and fantastic.

It would be pleasant to know more about the *Epigoni's* contents, and numerous traditions about the deeds of the sons of the Seven are preserved in Apollodorus and other late sources. But these traditions are divergent as well as numerous, and there are other early poems from which they might derive. The epic known as the *Alcmaeonis* (*E.G.F.* p. 139f.) dealt, as its very title indicates, with the career of Alcmaeon, the son of Amphiaraus, pledged by his departing father to matricide (see above, p. 27). The lyric poet Stesichorus wrote a long epic-like poem called *Eriphyle* which must have embracd pretty much the same material. Sophocles composed a drama known as the *Epigoni* (*Tr.G.F.* 4 183ff. Radt). The task of assigning the different strands of tradition found in later prose authors to these much earlier poets is both difficult and dangerous and cannot be attempted here.

6: The Cypria

Antiquity assigned this poem either to Homer (T 1-5) or to the Cypriot poet Stasinus (T 7-11). The delightful story that the impoverished Homer gave the poem to his son-in-law Stasinus, as a substitute for a dowry for his daughter (cf. T 1 and T 8), is probably a relatively late anecdote of a familiar kind, bringing together contemporary but differently aged practitioners of the same genre and intended to reconcile these alternative attributions. It is often alleged that the story dates back at least as far as Pindar, but the passage in question (T 1) may only be evidence that Pindar assigned to Homer a word or phrase which later writers recognised in the text of the *Cypria*. The linking of this to the dowry anecdote might be a later development. Herodotus 2.117 (T 5 = F 11) is the earliest extant writer to deny the *Cypria* to Homer: this need signify no more than that he too believed it was the work of Stasinus. On the work's date see above, p. 3ff.

Why did the epic bear the title *Cypria*? The most popular and convincing explanation (cf. T 9) talks in terms of Stasinus' place of origin and compares the epic known as *Naupactia* (*E.G.F.* pp. 145ff.) which has a name relating to the city where its author lived, rather than to its own content. This is so unusual a way of naming a poem that, from the seventeenth century at least onwards, some scholars have preferred to associate the title with Aphrodite, a goddess closely connected with Cyprus, whom we can infer to have played a major role in this poem. But that manner of devising a title for an epic has even less analogies than the first (with which compare also Thestorides of Phocaea's *Phocais* (*E.G.F.* p. 153)).

As with so many poems of the Epic Cycle, the *Cypria*'s main function, at least in its final stage, would seem to have been to supply the background presupposed by the *Iliad* and *Odyssey*. The numerous contradictions of those two epics' tone and ethos and the fewer inconsistencies in points of tradition need not tell against this interpretation of its purpose. The requirement to supply details of all the multifarious events that occurred before the start of the *Iliad* seems to have resulted in a work even more rambling (it amounted to eleven books), ramshackle and lacking in cohesion than the average, though a rather spurious unity was ingeniously imposed in F 1:

> Once upon a time the countless tribes <of mortals thronging about weighed down> the broad surface of the deep-bosomed earth. And Zeus, seeing this, took pity, and in his cunning mind he devised a plan to lighten the burden caused by mankind from the face of the all-nourishing earth, by fanning into flame the great strife that was the Trojan War, in order to alleviate the earth's burden by means of the death of men. So it was that the heroes were killed in battle at Troy and the will of Zeus was accomplished.

This fragment obviously occurred near the beginning of the poem, but there is no evidence that it constitutes the very opening lines and that the *Cypria* dispensed with the normal epic exordium appealing to the Muse which is attested for the *Iliad* and *Odyssey* as well as for the *Thebais* (F 1: see above, p. 23) and *mutatis mutandis* the *Little Iliad* (F 1: p. 61). The employment of the immemorial story-telling formula 'once upon a time...' is very unlike Homer (who avoids this feature so redolent of folk-tale) as is the ingenious exploitation of the folk-tale motif in which the gods take alarm at the growing numbers of mankind and resolve to reduce them by causing a catastrophe. Ancient near-eastern analogies for this motif can be cited. The phrase 'and the will of Zeus was accomplished' also occurs at the end of the *Iliad*'s proem (*Il.* 1.1-5) where it seems calculated to convey a rather complex effect, impressive but slightly mysterious, potentially reassuring but also potentially disturbing: Achilles' anger hurled down to the Underworld the mighty souls of many heroes, making their corpses a prey for dogs and birds to feast on – and the will of Zeus was accomplished. One might compare, from a very different time and milieu, this from the end of a Serbian folk-ballad: 'Thus the Tsar perished and with him all his soldiers, the seventy-seven thousand Serbs. And all that was holy and honourable and agreeable to God the Almighty'. We can see from the scholion on the Iliadic line, which is our source for F 1 of the *Cypria*, that the enigmatic nature of Homer's phrase caused controversy in antiquity, and was sometimes explained away by recourse to the identical phrase near the start of the *Cypria*. There, by contrast, Zeus' will or plan was perfectly straightforward (to reduce the burden on the earth). In fact one could not ask for a clearer illustration of the difference in ethos between Homer and the Epic Cycle.

Proclus tells us that Zeus deliberated with Themis as to <how to cause> the Trojan War. This was doubtless the immediate sequel to F 1. The Iliadic scholion which is our source for that fragment prefaces it with a story in which the earth, burdened by the weight of mankind and oppressed by the prevailing impiety, directly appeals to Zeus. He first eliminates many mortals by bringing about the Theban War and then, on the advice of Momus, the personification of blame or fault-finding, causes the Trojan War by having Thetis marry a mortal and give birth to the beautiful Helen, the cause of the war at Troy. 'The story is found in the *Cypria*' the scholion concludes, and cites F1. Several scholars therefore infer that Momus and the rest of the account occurred in that epic. But this story, though similar to the background implied by F 1, is clearly not perfectly compatible with it (our fragment leaves no room for an appeal by a personified Mother Earth or a Theban War as a preliminary stage of Zeus' plan; nor is Momus easy to fit in). The scholion's narrative must therefore have a different source to the *Cypria*.

Themis, goddess of righteousness, the first of the numerous significant personifications in the poem (see below, pp. 35 and 37f.), is an appropriate adviser to Zeus concerning his great plan to reduce mankind (more so than Momus in the alternative tradition). Her support confirms the rightness of the plan. Since Proclus next mentions the marriage of Peleus and Thetis, the result of Zeus' deliberations must have been precisely that marriage, and this is where F 2 comes in. For it tells us that Thetis had gratified Hera by rejecting Zeus' earlier sexual advances. Zeus in anger swore that Thetis, a goddess, would be punished by marriage to a mortal. Hera, presumably, showed her gratitude to Thetis by ensuring that the mortal in question would be the greatest then living and (cf. *Il.* 24.61 and Hes. fr. 211.3 MW) one particularly dear to the gods. The union, then, was 'overdetermined' in a way familiar from early Greek literature: the relatively personal and trite motives of Zeus and Hera move in the same direction as the loftier and more universal 'plan of Zeus'.

F 3 informs us of one of the gifts brought by the gods to the wedding of Peleus and Thetis: Chiron, the beneficent centaur who had reared Peleus, presented him with a spear made by Athena and Hephaestus. This spear would later be wielded by Achilles, the offspring of the marriage. (Apollod. 3.13.5 adds that Poseidon gave Peleus the immortal horses Balius and Xanthus; and this too may be from the *Cypria*.) But the event, we learn from Proclus, was marred by the arrival of Eris, a goddess personifying strife, who caused a quarrel about beauty between Athena, Hera and Aphrodite. If, as later writers state, Eris' malicious act was inspired by resentment at not receiving an invitation to the wedding, this episode too derives from a widely spread folk-tale motif, the deity cheated of honour or sacrifice, who takes revenge (one thinks of the Wicked Fairy's intervention at Sleeping Beauty's christening, or Artemis' sending of the Calydonian Boar to punish Oeneus). It has been argued that Eris simply turned up in the *Cypria's* account; that she need not have thrown the famous apple inscribed 'to the fairest' which is only explicitly attested in late authors and may be a Hellenistic invention; and that the judgement of Paris need not entail Eris' apple, the apple first visible in several early artistic depictions of the scene being explicable in a different way. This interpretation is both possible and much less natural.

The judgement of Paris, to which (says Proclus) Hermes led the three goddesses on Zeus' instruction, is only once explicitly mentioned by Homer (*Il.* 24.25ff.) but the *Iliad* on several occasions implies it, even if reluctant for various reasons to give it overt prominence. It is an extremely popular episode in later literature and art. One cannot guess with any likelihood which of the numerous details as to Paris' behaviour and the goddesses' bribes found in these later sources derive from the *Cypria*. We cannot even tell whether the poem parenthetically explained Paris' presence on Mt. Ida by the familiar tradition of his previous exposure and discovery by a shepherd, or whether this son of a king was watching his father's flocks as naturally as Aeneas, at a later stage in the same epic, guarded his family's cattle (below, p. 46f.). We do know, however, that the epic contained a description of Aphrodite's adornment, treated in terms reminiscent of Hera's beautification in the Iliadic *Deception of Zeus* (14.166ff.), Aphrodite's own in the *Homeric Hymn* to that deity (v.56ff.) and of the decking-out of Pandora in Hesiod's *Works and Days* (v.60ff.). According to F 4:

> She set on her skin the garments which the Graces and the Seasons had made and dyed in the flowers of spring-time, garments such as the Seasons wear, dyed in crocus and hyacinth and in the blooming violet and in the fair flower of the rose, sweet and fragrant, and in ambrosial flowers of the narcissus and the lily.
> Such were the garments fragrant in all seasons that Aphrodite put on herself.

A slightly later stage of the narrative seems to be represented in F 5:

> Laughter-loving Aphrodite, together with her attendants <...> plaiting fragrant garlands out of flowers of the earth they set them upon their heads, the goddesses with their bright headbands, the Nymphs and Graces, and with them golden Aphrodite, with fair song down the mountain of Ida rich in springs...

F 4 in particular has been deemed rather vacuously ornamental in comparison with the other epic instances of the motif of a goddess' self-beautification: the list of flowers meanders confusingly and the repetition of the word for 'flower' (*anthos*) three times in five lines does not display the archaic device of emphasis through duplication at its most elegant.

Proclus tells us that Paris' verdict in favour of Aphrodite was elicited by her promise of union with Helen. F 6 and F 7 of the *Cypria* deal respectively with the divergent destinies of the sons of Tyndareus and Leda:

> Castor was mortal, and the fate of death is allotted to him, but Polydeuces, scion of Ares, was immortal;

and the pursuit of Helen's mother Nemesis by Zeus:

> And after these two sons he begot as third offspring a girl, Helen, a wonder to mortals <...> Her once in the past fair-tressed Nemesis, after mingling in love, bore to Zeus king of the gods, by the dictates of a harsh destiny. For at first Nemesis tried to escape and was unwilling to mingle with him in a loving embrace, with him Zeus the father, son of Cronus, because her mind was oppressed with the feeling of shame and indignation. Therefore by land and by the limitless dark water of the sea she tried to escape, but Zeus pursued her, and was eager in his heart to get hold of her, as now she fled through the wave of the loud-roaring sea, transformed into the shape of a fish and set in tumult the vast waters, and now she fled across the Ocean river and the limits of the earth, and now again over the dry land with its fruitful clods. And all this time she kept changing into the various wild animals that the land nurtures in order to be finally quit of him.

F 6 might in theory have occurred in connection with any one of the numerous opportunities for mentioning the Dioscuri provided by the plot of the *Cypria*. But clearly it best fits their first and earliest mention. F 7 and its picture of Zeus' pursuit of Nemesis (with the ultimate purpose of begetting Helen) might be thought suitable for placing in the vicinity of Zeus' consultation with Themis as to his grand master-plan (above, p. 34f.). But it opens with an indubitable reference to the Dioscuri, who are at best tangential to that plan; and the Greek word *pote* ('once') used of the birth of Helen in v.2, tells against direct narrative. A particularly plausible suggestion locates both fragments in the context of the judgement of Paris, perhaps in a speech made to Paris by Aphrodite (Proclus' summary proceeds to relate various items of advice and instruction given by the goddess, and Paris' visit to Greece, where he is entertained first by the Dioscuri and then by Helen).

Homer characteristically omits from his epics the tradition that Peleus, before he could wed Thetis, had to capture her by force, wrestling with her on the sea-shore and holding on to her despite her shape-changing. The poet of the *Cypria*, though possessed by none of Homer's reluctance to include details redolent of folk-tale, seems likewise to have decided against incorporating this primeval detail within his poem: it would be at odds with his presumed picture (above, p. 34) of a Thetis *rewarded* by Hera with Peleus as husband and therefore unable to complain or resist. Instead, he transferred the motif, from its original and apposite association with the sea-sprite Thetis, to a rather less obviously appropriate connection with Nemesis, the personification of retribution. From F 8 we learn what happened when Zeus finally caught up with Nemesis: the two coupled in the form of male and female goose, and Nemesis later produced an egg from which Helen was born. The idea that Zeus, disguised as a swan, mated with Leda who gave birth to the famous egg from which Helen (and the Dioscuri) emerged, is infinitely more familiar to *us*: but its first explicit attestation is not until Euripides' *Helen*, and some would have it that it was Euripides who invented the story. The two versions are obviously closely linked, but it is not easy to say which came first and served as model for the other. A reconciling tradition, that Leda came across the egg and vicariously nurtured it and the children that emerged, is dateable quite early (it occurred in a poem by Sappho (fr. 166 LP)), so it may be that the *Cypria* replaced Leda with Nemesis in order to achieve further symbolic personification (compare above, p. 34). Leda certainly seems to have featured in our epic as mother of Castor and Polydeuces. F 6's picture of twins one immortal (because begotten by a god), one mortal (because begotten by a mortal) is another widely spread folk-tale motif which the *Iliad* rejects (in 3.243f. they are both dead), and the mortal and immortal in the *Cypria*'s case must have been Tyndareus and Zeus.

As hinted above, Proclus tells how the judgement was followed by Paris' construction of ships on Aphrodite's advice. His brother Helenus prophesied the future; Aphrodite instructed that her son Aeneas sail with Paris; Paris' sister Cassandra in turn prophesied the future. This arrant reduplication has created some disillusionment and disgust either with the *Cypria*'s repetitive poet or with Proclus as unreliable epitomiser. The episodes certainly have an unHomeric feel to them: Helenus and Cassandra are neither of them at all prominent in Homer's epics and when they are mentioned nothing is said of any prophetic powers (the raving prophetess is particularly alien to Homer's skilfully selective poetic world). But it must be said that in contrast to the *Iliad* and *Odyssey* (and like Virgil's *Aeneid*) the *Cypria* obviously laid great stress on oracles and prophecies (see for example below, pp. 42 and 45).

Paris (continues Proclus) sailed to Lacedaemon in Greece and was entertained first by the sons of Tyndareus and then by Menelaus in Sparta. Again the duplication is striking and may originally have had some point. A number of scholars have deduced from later sources that the banquet at which Castor and Polydeuces entertained Paris saw an ugly brawl break out between the Dioscuri and their cousins the sons of Aphareus, when the latter taunted the former over the unceremonious manner in which they had abducted Hilaeira and Phoebe (cousins of the sons of Aphareus) to be their brides. The two girls were certainly mentioned in the *Cypria* (F 9). It would have been an economic device if some such brawl had given Paris the idea of abducting Helen and determined the Dioscuri on their later fatal theft of the cattle of the sons of Aphareus (below, p. 40) to serve as dowry for their brides. We also know that the *Cypria* touched on Helen's earlier abduction (as a child) by Theseus, when her brothers the Dioscuri had been called on to rescue her (F 12). That detail too could have had a thematic relevance.

F 10 tells us that, in contrast to Homer (who gave Helen and Menelaus only one child (Hermione) and Helen and Paris none) the poet of the *Cypria* gave Helen and Menelaus a son Pleisthenes (who came with Helen to Cyprus on her flight) and Helen and Paris a son Aganus. Such proliferation of offspring characterises later epic as opposed to the severer world of Homer (see pp. 80 and 89). In his poems Helen's beauty and aura of mystery cannot be diminished by the presence of a whole brood of offspring; the illegitimate liaison of Helen and Paris must be distinguished from a real marriage by its literal sterility; and the sheerly practical question of what to do with Helen's children by Paris after Troy has fallen can be totally side-stepped.

As regards Paris' entertainment at Sparta we learn from Proclus that Helen received gifts from Paris and that Menelaus, on having to sail to Crete, left his wife with instructions to entertain Paris and his retinue appropriately until they departed. The untimely call to Crete recurs in later authors, and the extra detail in Apollod. *Epit.* 3.3 that Menelaus was required to attend his maternal grandfather's funeral probably derives from our epic. Menelaus' instructions to Helen seem inept in view of the sequel. That Proclus' summary saw fit to mention so seemingly trivial a detail might suggest that the *Cypria* stressed the perversity. At any rate, Aphrodite brought together Paris and Helen and after making love they sailed off at night taking a great deal of Menelaus' property with them (cf. *Il.* 3.70ff., 91ff., 282ff. etc.). So says Proclus, who continues with the statement that Hera, <resentful after the judgement of Paris,> sent a storm which drove the erring couple to Sidon: Paris sacked the city and then sailed back off to Troy where he celebrated his marriage to Helen. This portion of Proclus' summary raises one of the most thorny problems concerning the *Cypria*. For F 11 (that is Herodotus 2.117) states, by contrast, that Paris took only three days to bring Helen from Greece to Troy because he enjoyed a favourable breeze and a calm sea. How explain the contradiction? Many scholars have resorted to the likelihood that Proclus' summaries have occasionally been adjusted to bring their details into line with Homer's epics (see above, p. 7) but this does nothing to clarify the present difficulty; for the storm mentioned by Proclus does not feature in the relevant Homeric passages (*Il.* 6.289ff. and *Od.* 4.227ff.). Herodotus' own summary of these lines is rather misleading (he implies that Homer says Paris was forced to put in at Sidon) and it may be that his well-known contrast of the *Cypria*'s calm voyage with the Iliadic scheme has (in over-simplified form) influenced Proclus' phrasing.

Since the Dioscuri had intervened on an earlier occasion to rescue Helen from abduction (F 12), it was necessary to explain why they were powerless to help now and why they were absent from the Trojan expedition (cf. *Il.* 3.243f.). So Proclus observes that while Paris was bringing Helen to Troy, Castor and Polydeuces were detected by Idas and Lynceus, the sons of Aphareus, as they tried to rustle their cattle. The cattle-raid as heroic exploit is yet another popular folk-tale motif. A few lines of description from this part of the poem are preserved as F 13:

> Lynceus quickly sped to Taygetus, trusting in his swift feet. And climbing to the topmost part of the mountain he gazed over the whole island of Pelops, son of Tantalus, and swiftly the glorious hero espied with his formidably sharp eyes hidden within the hollow of an oak both of them, Castor the tamer of horses and Polydeuces winner of contests. So standing by the mighty oak he struck <...>.

The sequel as outlined by Proclus (and confirmed by several authors later than the *Cypria*) is that Castor was killed by Idas, and Lynceus and Idas by Polydeuces. F 14 adds the slightly sharper perspective that Castor was *speared* by Idas. Then (to revert to Proclus' summary) Zeus bestowed alternative immortality upon the Dioscuri (a detail also recounted in, for instance, *Od.* 11.300ff.).

Pindar's superb narrative of these events (*Nemean* 10.60ff.) seems to derive from the *Cypria*, though he characteristically recasts those details that might discredit the Dioscuri. In his account Castor is not lurking treacherously with his brother inside a hollow oak, but casually sitting on the stump of an oak-tree far from Polydeuces, who has to run to his aid when the two sons of Aphareus attack. The preternaturally lynx-sharp eyes of the appropriately named Lynceus are another of the features that set the *Cypria* apart from Homer's epics.

Proclus' résumé continues with the information that Iris brought the news of his wife's elopement to Menelaus (Iris was, then, messenger of the gods, as in the *Iliad*). Menelaus proceeded to confer with his brother Agamemnon concerning the expedition against Troy, and then moved on to visit Nestor. Nestor parenthetically related to him in a digression several mythical events: Epopeus' seduction of the daughter of Lycurgus and his consequent destruction; the story of Oedipus; the madness of Heracles; and the story of Theseus and Ariadne. Homer's epics often employ myths paradigmatically to point a moral, and the Iliadic Nestor on several occasions puts myths to this use. It is not difficult to see how the first and fourth of Nestor's tales in the *Cypria* might have furnished edifying precedents for the punishment of sexual escapades (for the early version of the Theseus and Ariadne story which concludes with the latter's killing by Artemis, see *Od.* 11.322ff. and Eur. *Hipp.* 339). The second and third tales are less obviously explicable in this light: perhaps we do not know enough of the relevant versions, perhaps Nestor's sense of relevance was deficient in comparison with the Iliadic standard (the accumulation of *exempla* is certainly without parallel in Homer). F 15 may conceivably belong to the same context; someone gave Menelaus the following pointed advice:

> I tell you, Menelaus, it is wine that the gods have devised as the best means for mortal men to disperse their cares.

Menelaus, Agamemnon and Nestor then proceeded through Greece gathering the leaders for the expedition. So says Proclus' summary which next presents as with some strikingly unHomeric details: Odysseus is unwilling to participate in the expedition and feigns madness, but is unmasked when, at Palamedes' prompting; Odysseus' son Telemachus is snatched up with a view to punishing Odysseus. The compressed narrative again becomes clearer in the light of later accounts which tell how Odysseus' assumed madness was manifested by his attempting to plough the sea-shore and sow it with salt, a ploy brought to an abrupt end when his infant son Telemachus was set down in the path of the plough. Madness (feigned or genuine) is strikingly absent from the Homeric epics; alien to them likewise is the notion that a hero would dishonourably seek to avoid battle (like Amphiaraus before the Seven's assault on Thebes: see p. 27). Only heroic anger and resentment such as Achilles' is allowed by Homer as a legitimate motive for such abstinence. Finally the figure of Palamedes goes totally without mention in either the *Iliad* or *Odyssey*. Later authors explain that it was the present thwarting of Odysseus' scheme that inspired the hostility which finally led to Palamedes' death (below, p. 48).

By contrast, the next section of Proclus' summary is remarkably consistent with the Iliadic scheme of things: the Greek force assembled at Aulis and made sacrifice. An omen involving a snake and sparrows was witnessed, and the seer Calchas drew conclusions for the future. All this fits with the account given by Odysseus in *Il*. 2.303ff. (the snake's devouring of nine sparrows before it is miraculously turned to stone by Zeus portends as many years of war before final success in the tenth) as well as matching the *Cypria's* predilection for prophecies and the miraculous.

A complete contrast follows with the markedly unHomeric content of the next section of Proclus' résumé. The Greek forces sailed to the land of Teuthrania, put in there, and proceeded to ravage it under the misapprehension that it was Troy. Telephus <the king of the region> sallied out, killed Thersander son of Polyneices and <one of the Greek leaders> and was in turn himself wounded by Achilles. Some scholars have ingeniously tried to detect indirect allusions to this abortive expedition in the narrative of the *Iliad* but they have rightly failed to carry

The Cypria 43

conviction. It may well be that the author of the *Cypria* invented the Teuthranian expedition as a prelude to the Trojan War proper. He may also have created many of the details that characterise the former by transferring motifs from the opening episode of the latter; for, as reconstructed from later writers, the Teuthranian episode reads like a doublet of the initial invasion of Troy. His aim was presumably to diversify the plot of his epic and introduce battle-scenes that the Trojans' long refusal to fight would largely deny him once he had brought his Greek forces to Troy.

<Recognising their error> the Greeks sailed away from Mysia only to be beset by a storm (Proclus continues). Their forces were thereby scattered and Achilles put in at the island of Scyros where he married Deidameia, daughter of Lycomedes. F 16 of the *Cypria* comes handily to our aid here. It tells us that the poem gave a rather more refined account of the name of Achilles' son Neoptolemus than we get in Homer, to wit that his grandfather Lycomedes called him Pyrrhus ('red-haired'), and that Neoptolemus was the name given him by Phoenix (Achilles' tutor, as in the *Iliad*) because his father Achilles was young (*neos*) when he began to fight in war (*ptolemein*). The idea of naming a child after the qualities or achievements of one of its parents is quite common in early Greek poetry (e.g., according to some, Telemachus was so named because his father Odysseus was far away (*têle-*) fighting a battle (*machê*) at Troy).

The detail of Achilles' putting in at Scyros is not fully intelligible without reference to a further tradition. At an earlier stage Peleus, aware that his son was fated to die at Troy, had hidden him away on the isle of Scyros. Here he was brought up among girls and dressed as such until Odysseus, searching for the hero without whom (according to an oracle) Troy could not fall, ferreted him out by a famous device. Together with Phoenix and Nestor he went to Scyros and saw to it that a number of weapons along with baskets and equipment for weaving were set down before the young girls' quarters. Alone of the 'girls' Achilles picked up the weapons and was thereby detected. A late source attributes this story to poets of the Epic Cycle (*Fr. incert. loc.* 4) and most scholars assume that the *Cypria* was meant, but there are other possibilities (below, p. 64). The same source tells us that these Cyclic poets also related how

Achilles slept with Deidameia and begot Neoptolemus while he was hidden among the girls.

To return to Proclus: he next relates how Telephus, following the dictates of an oracle, arrived at Argos and was healed by Achilles on the understanding that he would then guide the expedition to Troy. Once again it is hard not to be struck by the unHomerically important role assigned to prophecies and oracular pronouncements and to folk-tale motifs, like 'the wounder shall heal', which underlie this part of the poem. How many of the subsidiary details later found in Euripides' *Telephus* (Austin, *Nova Fragmenta Euripidea* pp. 66ff.) were already present in the *Cypria*'s treatment it is not easy to say.

Proclus then summarises events during the expedition's second gathering at Aulis: Agamemnon's ill-timed boast that he had surpassed Artemis in the skill with which he shot a deer; the angry goddess' penning-up of the fleet at Aulis with stormy winds; Calchas' explanation of her wrath and his demand for the sacrifice of Iphigeneia as appeasement; the summoning of Iphigeneia to the Greek camp under the pretext of marriage to Achilles; and the attempt at sacrifice thwarted by Artemis, who substituted a deer and transported Iphigeneia to the land of the Taurians. All of this again achieves a very unHomeric impression. The primitive concept of the sacrifice of a young virgin to achieve an expedition's success is totally alien to the ethos of Homer's poems, which, indeed, preserve a sedulous silence as to the existence of Iphigeneia. In *Iliad* 9 Agamemnon mentions three daughters as part of his list of inducements to Achilles to renounce his anger, and a very idiosyncratic set of names they bear in contrast to what we might expect after reading, for instance, the Athenian tragedians on the family of Agamemnon. Chrysothemis, Laodice and Iphianassa (145 = 287) are Homer's three daughters of Agamemnon. Their melodious and etymologically symbolic names may have been invented *ad hoc* by the poet. Laodice and Iphianassa were identified by some later writers with Electra and Iphigeneia, but Homer's original plan may have been to distract his audience's minds from the grim stories attached to those unhappy heroines. Certainly his Iphianassa is still alive in the ninth year of the war, and we learn from F 17 that the poet of the *Cypria* distinguished her from Iphigeneia by giving Agamemnon four daughters (the remaining two presumably Electra and Chrysothemis). The miraculous substitution of the deer for Iphigeneia is another of those folk-tale motifs for which Homer has little time. Even at this stage the *Cypria*'s poet seems to have given his epic's plot further twists and elaborations before allowing the Greeks to reach Troy. Proclus says their force put in at Tenedos (no resistance or fighting is specifically mentioned). While the Greeks were feasting on Tenedos, Philoctetes was bitten by a water-snake and the stench of his wound grew so dreadful that he had to be abandoned (on the isle of Lemnos). Thus was his absence from all but the tenth year of the Trojan War explained (cf. *Il* 2.718ff.). A hero with an incurable but not fatal wound is markedly unHomeric. Achilles was summoned late (Proclus proceeds) and quarrelled with Agamemnon. Heroic quarrels (such as that between the two self-same heroes which opens the *Iliad*) were a common motif of early epic. Some scholars have tried to identify the *Cypria*'s disagreement with one or other of these (e.g. that at *Od.* 8.72ff.) but the likeliest amplification of the detail in Proclus' summary bases itself on Sophocles' lost tragedy *The Fellow Feasters* (*Syndeipnoi*: see *Tr.G.F.* 4.425ff. Radt). Here, it seems, Achilles quarrelled with the Greeks on Tenedos because he was invited late to a feast.

F 19 may be mentioned next because it certainly suggests a further retardation of his plot by the *Cypria*'s poet. It tells how King Anius of Delos tried to persuade the Greek forces to stay with him because divine knowledge had been granted him and he foresaw nine unsuccessful years of war before the final victory (again the penchant for the oracular and prophetic manifests itself: see p. 38f.). Scholars have perhaps been excessively ready to infer from other sources that the *Cypria* too exploited the further detail that Anius' daughters the Oenotropoi supplied the Greek forces at Troy with food (rescuing them, by one account, from a serious famine). Nothing of this is in our fragment, which merely states that Anius promised his daughters would maintain the Greeks *in Delos*. The three daughters with their etymologically significant names – Oeno ('wine-girl'), Spermo ('seed-girl'), Elais ('oil-girl') – are nevertheless a further token of the poem's liking for the marvellous and the romantically picturesque.

At last the Greeks reached Troy. Proclus tells us that their landing was opposed by the Trojans, and that Protesilaus was killed by Hector. Protesilaus' role in the epic is amplified by F 18, which reminds us that, when the Greeks were hesitating to disembark on Trojan soil, Protesilaus, appropriately for his name, was the *first* who dared to *leap* ashore. Apollod. *Epit.* 3.29f. completes the pattern of the story with the detail that Thetis ordered Achilles not to be the first to set foot on shore, for the first such person was doomed to die. The *Cypria*'s fondness for such prophecies and for such ancient motifs as the sacrifice of the initiator's life to ensure an enterprise's success encourages the hypothesis that our poem contained this detail too. F 18 also names Protesilaus' wife as Polydora daugher of Oeneus.

Returning to Proclus we learn that Achilles' slaying of Cycnus ensured the rout of the Trojans. The Greeks recovered their corpses.

Proclus' next item, the Greeks' embassy to Troy requesting the return of Helen and the property stolen with her, was a popular theme in a good deal of later art and literature (it is already implied at *Il.* 3.205ff., where Odysseus and Menelaus are mentioned as ambassadors). The request being refused (says Proclus), the Greeks invested the city and then ravaged the countryside and the surrounding towns. After this, Achilles was desirous of seeing Helen, and Aphrodite and Thetis brought them together. This is an extremely unHomeric episode. The mention of Aphrodite surely indicates that the bringing together was sexual: the bravest hero and the fairest heroine appropriately united, just as (according to another tradition) they lived together on the island of Leuce after their deaths. That version was probably the inspiration for the *Cypria*'s idea of an earlier encounter (note that the *Hesiodic Catalogue of Women* (Hes. fr. 204.87ff, MW) claims that Achilles would have married Helen had he been old enough to compete as a suitor). The romantic elaboration is characteristic of much of the Epic Cycle. Proclus' next detail probably relates directly to what has gone before: the Greek forces revolted and tried to go home but Achilles checked them – presumably because of his meeting with the direct cause of the war. This is superficially similar to Odysseus' restraining of the host at *Il.* 2.169ff. but really very different, if purely selfish and romantic motives underlay Achilles' action.

Much of what comes next in Proclus' summary reads like a definite attempt on the part of the poet to prepare for events in the *Iliad*. For we are told that Achilles drove off the cattle of Aeneas and sacked Lyrnessus and Pedasus together with many of the surrounding cities. Two passages in the *Iliad* presuppose this theft of cattle (for whose status as heroic act see above, p. 40f.) followed by the destruction of the two cities: 2.688ff. and 16.56f. And yet an independent fragment from our poem seems to suggest that the fit between Homer's and this epic was not completely snug and comfortable. For F 21, as naturally approached, states that the *Cypria*'s Achilles captured Briseis, the slave-girl so crucial to the Iliadic wrath-theme, from Pedasus. In the *Iliad*, of course, she comes from Lyrnessus. Only a strained interpretation of the fragment's wording can avoid this inconcinnity.

Next in Proclus' summary comes Achilles' murder of Troilus. Like Cassandra and Helenus (see above, p. 38) Troilus is a child of Priam whom Homer mentions very sparingly indeed. His death at Achilles' hands becomes a very popular motif in later literature and art, but is variously represented. Sometimes he is depicted as killed in ambush or slaughtered on the altar of Apollo; sometimes his killing is associated with Achilles' sighting of Polyxena, with whom Achilles falls in love; sometimes Achilles himself is given homosexual feelings for Troilus. All and any of which associations are quite incompatible with the heroic world as constructed by Homer.

After this detail Proclus proceeds with an account of how Patroclus sold Lycaon, another son of Priam, into slavery in Lemnos and how, in the distribution of booty, Achilles received Briseis while Agamemnon got Chryseis. Once again there is the impression of a preparation for significant motifs in the *Iliad* (on Lycaon cf. 21.34ff.). F 22 reveals that the *Cypria* had an explanation for Chryseis' presence in Hypoplacian Thebes (her place of capture): she was attending a festival of Artemis. This detail looks very much like an attempt to answer the question 'Why does the *Iliad* (1.366) present Chryseis as captured in a city other than Chryse, to which she is linked by name as well as father?' A scholion on the relevant line of the *Iliad* gives additional details: Chryseis was visiting Iphinoe, daughter of Actor; Athena <foreseeing the wrath> had forbidden Achilles to sack Chryse. These may also derive from the *Cypria*.

Next the *Cypria* treated the death of Palamedes. Proclus' lapidary statement to this effect conceals beneath its surface a remarkably un-Homeric treatment of a literally unHomeric figure (cf. above, p. 42). From F 20 we learn more about the mode of death: Palamedes was drowned by Diomedes and Odysseus while out fishing. The collaboration of Diomedes and Odysseus is Iliadic, but further from Homeric values one could hardly go than this tale of the cowardly and treacherous murder (to such an undignified background) of a fellow-Greek. (Fishing in Homer is always a last resort due to the absence of a more heroic diet of meat: we recall that some authors mention a famine during the Trojan War (see above p. 45).) Later writers attribute a different, though no less Machiavellian, means of securing Palamedes' death to Odysseus. It is hardly surprising that the sympathetic treatment of the latter in the *Odyssey* has no room for mention of his rival from earlier days. The reason for Palamedes' absence from the *Iliad* is not so immediately obvious, but he seems in origin to be a type of the culture-hero, the *prôtos heuretês* or *primus inventor* of such aspects of civilisation as the alphabet and draughts, and, given this flavour of folk-lore, profoundly unHomeric.

Proclus' summary of the *Cypria* ends with two items as lapidary as his notice of Palamedes' death, but in this case, unfortunately, we have no fragments to lend independent illumination. What he says is that at the end of the poem there was mention of the will or plan of Zeus (the same two words as at F 1.7 and *Il*. 1.5: above, p. 34) to lighten the Trojan burden by causing Achilles to revolt from his duties to the Greek alliance; and a catalogue of the allies who fought on the Trojan side. One infers for the first detail some sort of intended link with the events of *Iliad* Book 1, though an accurate summary of the latter would state that Zeus wanted to honour Achilles rather than help the Trojans by making Achilles withdraw. Perhaps (as in F 1) the *Cypria* revised the Iliadic scheme; or perhaps Proclus' summary has been altered to bring it closer to the *Iliad*'s version than it originally was.

The catalogue of Trojan allies is not quite so problematic, especially if interpreted in light of the catalogue of the same given by Apollod. *Epit*. 3.34f. which is prefaced by the information that the allies only arrived during the ninth year of the war. This would neatly explain the catalogue's otherwise strangely late position within the *Cypria*. A

The Cypria

catalogue of Trojan allies also occurs at *Il.* 2.816ff. but that is under a cloud of suspicion for a number of independent reasons, and the simplest deduction from Proclus is that the poet of the *Cypria* included a catalogue of Trojan allies because the *Iliad* in the form known to him was deficient in this respect (cf. below, p. 85 on a similar problem within the *Telegony*).

We have already considered above those fragments that can be located with certainty or by conjecture within the framework of the *Cypria*'s plot. Some, however, are quite unplaceable. This is true, for instance, of F 23, which tells us that the poem specified Eurydice as the name borne by the wife of Aeneas, a hero who featured on several occasions during the poem. F 24 reveals that someone said to somebody else at some point in the epic:

> It is Zeus the god, who did this and who brought all these things to fruition, that you are unwilling to name: for where there is fear there, too, is shame.

A similarly unassignable generalisation is provided by F 25:

> Foolish the man who, while he kills the father, leaves the sons behind.

F 26 shows that the *Cypria* mentioned the Gorgons and their island of Sarpedon (in what context we cannot hope to guess):

> And conceiving by him she bore to him the Gorgons, baleful monsters, who dwelt on Sarpedon, by the deep-edying Ocean, a rocky isle.

Finally, the intriguing F 27 brings the surprising news that the *Cypria*'s poet had Polyxena die after being wounded by Odysseus and Diomedes at the sack of Troy, and be buried by Neoptolemus. Surprising, because this version of events is so very different from the *Sack of Troy*'s more familiar tradition that Neoptolemus sacrificed her to his father's shade (below, p. 73); surprising also because we have no real reason to suppose that the main narrative of our epic proceeded anything like so far as the sack of Troy. Presumably this detail featured proleptically or parenthetically.

Scholars have also wanted to assign to the *Cypria* a number of unHomeric traditions that are so wide-spread and tenacious in later accounts that they must (it is felt) have featured in some early and influential epic. These include the notion of an oath by the suitors of Helen to come to recover her should she ever be abducted from her chosen husband; and the picture of Achilles reared (like his father) by the centaur Chiron and fed on the innards and marrow of wild beasts, so that he sympathetically absorbed their speed and strength.

7: The Aethiopis

This epic, in five books, was attributed to Arctinus of Miletus (see above, p. 13). For reasons which will later become clear, it is best to start by considering Proclus' résumé of the poem's contents and leave the question of fragments until the end.

It is dangerous to generalise about the structure of an epic, the original of which has disappeared so completely. But it may be permissible to suggest, in the light of the evidence supplied by Proclus, that the poem comprised two halves each dealing with the exploits of a newly-arrived Trojan ally: the first Penthesileia the Amazon, the second Memnon the Aethiopian prince. The latter half gave the whole epic its name (though one should note that there is some evidence for the existence of an epic called the *Amazonia*, which may be an alternative name for the *Aethiopis*).

The poem seems to have begun, then, with the arrival of the Amazon Penthesileia to fight on the Trojans' behalf. Proclus says she was the daughter of Ares <the war-god particularly associated with Thrace> and herself Thracian by birth. Later authors fill in the details of Penthesileia's background and parentage (e.g. Apollod. *Epit*. 5.1 identifies her mother as Otrera and says she had accidentally killed <the Amazon> Hippolyta and came to Priam for purification). What should particularly be stressed here is the markedly unHomeric nature of this personage. The idea of a female warrior, presumably (as in later authors) at the head of a whole army of female warriors, is contrary to Homer's picture of the world, where women are accorded a small number of strictly normal roles (wife, mother, or the like) and even the notion of a prophetess (as with Cassandra: above, p. 38) must be excluded.

Even more unHomeric was the sequel in the *Aethiopis*: Proclus tells us Penthesileia enjoyed the traditional epic *aristeia* or display of valour before being killed by Achilles. (Apollod. *Epit*. 5.1 specifies Machaon <the physician son of Asclepius> as one of her victims and this detail may come from our epic: cf. below, p. 63.) The Trojans buried her and then Achilles slew Thersites because that warrior had insulted and taunted him with an allegation of love for Penthesileia. How seriously this charge was intended in the original we can no longer say. Later writers (in particular Quintus of Smyrna (in his third century AD epic on events following the *Iliad*) 1.718.ff.) depict Achilles as feeling pity and love for the newly-killed Amazon and then killing the abusive Thersites over her corpse. Unless Proclus' résumé has for some reason altered the original sequence of events, Thersites' offence and punishment occurred in the *Aethiopis* some time after Penthesileia's death. Even so, the romantic emotion alleged is strikingly unlike anything in Homer.

The unloveable figure of Thersites, it might be argued, is, by contrast, relatively Homeric (cf. his drubbing at the hands of Odysseus in *Il.* 2.212ff.). But consider Proclus' testimony as to the consequences of his killing: a quarrel broke out among the Greeks because of his murder. This does not sound very like the universally unpopular victim of *Il.* 2.274f. whose punishment induces general satisfaction. A scholion on *Il.* 2.212 refers to the unHomeric tradition of an Aetolian Thersites of *noble birth*, son of Oeneus' brother Agrius and thereby kinsman of Oeneus' grandson Diomedes. And Quintus of Smyrna (see above) 1.767ff. tells us that Diomedes, alone of the Greeks, was angered at his kinsman Thersites' death. It is not, indeed, perfectly easy to combine all these traditions or derive them from the *Aethiopis*. But they do at the least provide a salutary reminder of the possibility of an unHomeric treatment of Thersites in our poem.

Proclus next tells us that in consequence of his killing of Thersites, Achilles sailed to the island of Lesbos and by sacrificing to Apollo, Artemis and Leto was purified at Odysseus' hands from the <pollution caused by the> murder. This detail too is very different from Homer, who chooses not to give much scope at all in his epics to the primitive and important concepts of pollution and purification. The three deities mentioned by Proclus in his summary constitute a frequently mentioned trio, but this very passage is our sole piece of evidence for Apollo as recipient of offerings in a context of purification and the same is true of Artemis (though both are elsewhere connected with purity in general, and the goddess traditionally heals victims of madness). Perhaps the author of the *Aethiopis* was acquainted with a cult of the three deities on Lesbos. Odysseus' role as human purifier is also strictly unHomeric, though his accompanying of Achilles to Lesbos reminds one of his role in the voyage to Chryse at *Il*. 1.308ff. and both epics may have portrayed him as instrumental in quelling strife among the Greeks.

What we speculatively identified above (p. 51) as the second major episode in the *Aethiopis* opened with the arrival of Memnon, who (Proclus says) was the son of Eos <goddess of the dawn>. Apollod. *Epit.* 5.3 adds (what is anyway well known) that his father was Tithonus. Homer shows awareness of the story that Eos abducted and married the Trojan mortal Tithonus, but says nothing of the most famous aspect of the tale, that she acquired immortality (forgetting, however, to get everlasting youth at the same time) for her paramour. The idea of easily acquired immortality for the favourites of divinities is, as we have already seen in connection with the *Thebais* (above, p. 26), very un-Homeric. Proclus adds that Memnon arrived to help the Trojans wearing armour made by Hephaestus. He was thus presented as a fit match for Achilles, whose mother Thetis had persuaded Hephaestus to manufacture armour for her son at *Il*. 18.457ff. The evidence of Vergil's *Aeneid* (8.383f., where Venus says to her husband Vulcan *te filia Nerei, | te potuit lacrimis Tithonia flectere coniunx*) has reasonably enough been taken as suggesting that the *Aethiopis* mentioned a similar scene of persuasion by Eos.

The next portion of Proclus' summary states that Thetis gave her son advance information as to events concerning Memnon. In the *Iliad* Thetis often prophesies with divine foreknowledge the fate of Achilles (note especially 18.94ff.) and something analogous presumably occurred in our epic. In Proclus' résumé, Achilles' death follows so speedily after his killing of Memnon that the summary phrase 'events concerning Memnon' might easily include death (and perhaps even Achilles' eventual immortalisation).

Battle was joined, says Proclus, and Antilochus was killed by Memnon. From later writers (especially Pindar *Pyth*. 6.28ff.) it is inferred that Antilochus died saving his father Nestor from the Aethiopian prince's onslaught. We have considered above (p. 4) at a very general level the relationship between the *Aethiopis*' exploitation of this tradition and the analogous episode in *Il.* 8.130ff. Many of the episodes in the *Aethiopis* that follow (as presented in Proclus' summary) seem to display a like relationship with other parts of the *Iliad*; but we have no space to consider the question in appropriate detail: the issue of priority is very complex but probably resolvable on the same terms as apply with the episode in *Iliad* 8. Vergil's *Aeneid* Book Eight has already been cited once (p. 53) to cast light on our lost epic. Its picture (v.560ff.) of Evander's farewell to his son Pallas, who leaves to fight for Aeneas and to meet ultimate death on the battlefield, may likewise be indebted to some equivalent scene of farewell between Nestor and the similarly fated Antilochus, just as several passages of Latin poetry, which presuppose a tradition where Nestor laments the paradoxical destiny that has made him outlive his son, probably go back to the *Aethiopis*.

Next in Proclus' summary comes Achilles' slaying of Memnon <in revenge for the death of Antilochus>. Eos then requested from Zeus and received immortality for her dead son. Presumably this is to be related to her earlier (flawed) obtaining of immortality for her husband Tithonus (above, p. 53), though it would be hard to prove which instance of the motif came first. One would also assume, given the dawn-goddess' inevitable association with the East and her son's consequent origin in an eastern and exotic country, that Memnon's immortal existence was located in an eastern context.

Several vase-paintings are often called in aid to help elaborate this portion of our epic. Firstly, a large group of vases shows a so-called *Psychostasia*: the souls of Achilles and Memnon are weighed in the scales in the presence of their mothers Thetis and Eos, each of whom pleads on behalf of her own son. A lost tragedy of Aeschylus (see *Tr.G.F.* 3 p. 374f. Radt) is alleged by later writers (especially Plutarch) to have contained a similar scene in which Zeus held the scales; and since the vases stylistically post-date the production of the relevant tragedy, the most popular explanation of the available evidence is that vases and tragedy alike were independently reflecting an incident in the *Aethiopis*. This may be so, but caution must always be applied in assessing the complex relationships between art and literature. In the present case the vases are strangely divergent as to the identity of the deity holding the scales – it is not always Zeus, who is not invariably depicted as present.

This is unexpected if they all presuppose the *Aethiopis* as ultimate source. Furthermore, one should not necessarily infer an epic passage in which both mothers appeared to plead for their sons: this might merely be the vase-painter's vivid way of expressing their natural concern. Similarly a second group of vases, depicting the combat of Achilles and Memnon with each hero supported by the presence of his mother, need not imply, even if dependent upon the *Aethiopis*, that the epic showed the mothers as literally present on the battlefield. A third group, which shows Eos snatching her son's corpse from the field of battle, presents no particular difficulties and may well reflect the *Aethiopis*' scheme of events. By contrast a fourth and final group which has often been interpreted as the transportation af Memnon's corpse by the brothers Hypnos and Thanatos (personified Sleep and Death) is intensely problematic if connected with our epic. For all sorts of problems start then to arise: if the *Aethiopis* presented Memnon as winning immortality, why should Death be involved at all? One would expect Eos herself to transport her son to his immortal existence (or if not Eos, then, as in the description of the event in Quintus of Smyrna's epic 2.570ff., the winds). It may be that the vases' Hypnos and Thanatos have been transferred, as it were, from *Il.* 16.670ff. where, much more logically, they are depicted as carrying the corpse of Sarpedon back to his homeland of Lycia for burial. This is, at any rate, a salutary reminder of the difficulties involved in invoking the aid of art for the reconstruction of lost epics.

Let us return to Proclus' summary. After killing Memnon Achilles routed the Trojans; but, being caught up with them when they fled within the walls of Troy, he himself was killed by Paris and Apollo. The location of this death at Troy's Scaean Gate is added by Apollod. *Epit.* 5.3 which fits well with Hector's dying prophecy of Achilles' death at *Il.* 22.359f. (there too the collaboration of Apollo and Paris is mentioned). Apollodorus specifies that Achilles died from a wound in the heel, and this raises the interesting but difficult question whether this too derives from the *Aethiopis* and whether that epic already contained the famous motif of Achilles' heel, the single and sole vulnerable part of his body.

We should first clear our minds by stressing that an invulnerable Achilles is yet another of the motifs indebted to folk-lore which Homer explicitly eschews. His Achilles is indeed capable of being wounded (see *Il.* 21.166ff., 568ff.), and Homer would not wish to diminish the heroic stature of any of his characters by exempting them so easily from the omnipresent risk of death which is one of the great themes of his *Iliad*. No extant literary source mentions the famous detail of Thetis' dipping of the baby Achilles in the River Styx (to render him invulnerable) before Statius' *Achilleid* (1.134f.) in the first century AD, and there is no evidence of it from visual art before Hellenistic times. (The tradition that Thetis sought to render her infant son *immortal* by burning away his mortal parts occurs as early as Apollonius of Rhodes' *Argonautica* (4.869ff.) in the third century BC but does not necessarily entail the tradition of invulnerability.) Partial invulnerability is an exceedingly wide-spread motif that has a very primitive ring to it. The lesser hero Telemonian Ajax was portrayed as invulnerable by the time of Aeschylus, at least, and probably by the time of our own epic (see below, p. 58) and it is hard not to believe that the greater hero's invulnerability preceded his.

Proclus informs us that a fierce battle arose over Achilles' corpse which was, however, brought safely to the ships by Ajax, while Odysseus kept the Trojans off in a rearguard action. Apollod. *Epit.* 5.4 adds the details that Ajax killed the Trojan Glaucus in this action (this tradition recurs in other late authors and on a Chalcidian vase that is no longer extant) and gave orders for Achilles' armour to be carried separately off to the ships. It is likelier than not that these elaborations derive from the *Aethiopis*. The rescuing of the arms and the division of responsibilities between Ajax and Odysseus (each of whom is given a plausible case for any future judgement) neatly prepares for the next major stage of the story, the dispute over the arms of Achilles.

But first, Proclus tells us, the Greeks buried Antilochus and laid out the body of Achilles. Then Thetis arrived with the Muses and her sisters <the daughters of the Old Man of the Sea> and lamented her son. These details are also to be found in the account of Achilles' funeral at *Od.* 24.42ff., part of the so-called 'Second Nekyia' (see below, p. 85). The chronological relationship between that episode and our epic is quite uncertain. The picture of the Muses arriving to lament a mortal man (however distinguished he be) is very striking and unusual.

After this, Proclus' résumé continues, Thetis snatched her son, (or, presumably, his immortal part) from the funeral pyre and carried him off away to the Isle of Leuce (see above, p. 46). The contrived parallels between the careers of Achilles and Memnon (see above, p. 53) seem here to be continued to their logical conclusion: Memnon was granted immortality in the East and Achilles is now guaranteed a like existence on 'the White Island'. In each case the contrast with the austerity of the Homeric poems, where even the greatest heroes must die and the ghost of Achilles laments his fate in the Underworld (*Od.* 11.488ff.), is immense. Later authors concur in allowing Achilles a privileged existence after his death, but place him in other supposedly suitable locales – the Isles of the Blessed or the Elysian Plain.

Proclus' summary next tells us that the Greeks heaped up a funerary mound in Achilles' honour. There need be no inconsistency between this and the foregoing account of immortalisation: Greek myth reports other grave-mounds for mortals who have enjoyed apotheosis, and the famed tumulus of Achilles on the Troad's sea-shore required an explanation. Funeral Games for Achilles followed: such games are a familiar epic and poetic motif from *Iliad* 23's for Patroclus onwards. Apollod. *Epit.* 5.5 contains details as to which heroes were victorious in which contests, and these may come from the *Aethiopis*.

The final element in Proclus' résumé is the strife that broke out between Odysseus and Ajax over the arms of Achilles. But the only fragment of the *Aethiopis* which we possess deals with the suicide of Ajax that was the ultimate consequence of that strife. And yet the only reference to this suicide which we find in Proclus falls within his summary of the *Little Iliad* (see below, p. 62f.). It follows that Proclus has omitted the final section of the *Aethiopis* as a doublet and chosen to preserve only the *Little Iliad's* account of Ajax's end. There were various versions current in antiquity as to how the arms of Achilles were adjudged. We know that the *Little Iliad's* variant talked in terms of eaves-dropping on two Trojan girls (see below, p. 61f.). Another version (found, for instance, in Pindar *Nem.* 8.26f.) pictured the Greeks as electing a panel of judges to decide the issue. This seems the simplest solution and may, therefore, be the oldest version: it does not follow that it was what the *Aethiopis* adopted. A third account (cited, e.g., by a scholion on *Od.* 11.547) had the Greeks consult Trojan prisoners of war as to whether Odysseus or Ajax was the braver and more deserving of Achilles' arms: perhaps this was the *Aethiopis'* version (see further below, p. 62).

The actual fragment of the *Aethiopis* mentioned above deals with the precise time at which Ajax, disappointed in his hopes of receiving Achilles' armour, killed himself. The word used in the *Aethiopis* was *orthros*, which in early Greek refers to the last part of the night but later came to mean the dawn. This discrepancy seems to have been noticed by the Alexandrian scholar Aristarchus (cf. above, p. 4) who may be the source for the fragment in question.

Aeschylus in his lost tragedy *Thrêssai* (the *Thracian Women*) seems to have described the difficulty Ajax encountered in committing suicide because of his invulnerability (*Tr.G.F.* 3F 83 Radt). This leads one to wonder whether the *Aethiopis* mentioned the tradition of the invulnerable Ajax. As with Achilles (see above, p. 55f.), Homer has no time for an unwoundable Ajax (on the contrary: see *Il.* 14.402ff. and 23.822f.). Later authors derive the hero's invulnerability from the effect of sympathetic magic when, as an infant, he was enwrapped in Heracles' impenetrable lion-skin. That story seems to be as old as 'Hesiod' (fr. 250 MW) and to be implied (though not directly related) by Pindar *Isthm.* 6.36ff. It is often argued that Ajax was originally conceived as a giant, and as such he would be appropriately regarded as invulnerable. One would not be surprised, then, if he was so presented in the *Aethiopis*.

Finally, we must consider a 'spurious' fragment, two hexameters cited as an alternative ending for the *Iliad* by a scholion upon its last line (24.804):

> So they at any rate busied themselves over the funeral of Hector;
> and there came an Amazon, the daughter of great-hearted Ares
> who slays men.

These lines have frequently been regarded as the *opening* of the *Aethiopis*, but this is not what our source for them says they are, and it passes belief that any epic could ever have opened in such a casual and off-hand way. Another popular interpretation of the lines is that they are intended to link the *Iliad* and the *Aethiopis*: this view, too, is rather more difficult to sustain than is often realised; but at least it concedes that (by definition) the two verses in question cannot be a fragment of the latter epic.

8: The Little Iliad

The above title is the name given to an epic in four books by Lesches of Mytilene, which occupies a position in Proclus' summary of the Epic Cycle after Arctinus' *Aethiopis* and before his *Sack of Troy*. If we had only Proclus' testimony to go by, we should doubtless assume that the plot of each epic followed seamlessly on from that of the last. But numerous fragments of the *Little Iliad* seem to indicate that it encompassed events falling within the sack of Troy (below, p. 68ff.); and the only securely attested fragment of the *Aethiopis* deals with the death of Ajax (above, p. 58f.), an event that falls outside Proclus' summary of that poem. Most scholars have therefore concluded that Arctinus' *Aethiopis*, with his *Sack of Troy* on the one hand, and Lesches' *Little Iliad* on the other, overlapped very considerably in subject-matter: the two poets were each responsible for a different attempt to supply a sequel to the contents of the *Iliad*. Proclus' summary, in its characteristic way (see p. 7), has deliberately eliminated the overlapping material to produce the impression of a single coherent narrative.

This is the most widely held and convincing explanation of the existing phenomena. But one may mention an alternative approach, quite popular with German scholars at the turn of the century, which reduced the three epics supposedly distinguished above to one, the *Little Iliad*, of which the *Aethiopis* was an earlier portion (compare the Odyssean *Telemachy*), the *Sack of Troy* a later episode. This interpretation has some evidence compatible with it: in particular the relatively large number of fragments cited from the *Little Iliad* (c.25), the vanishingly small number cited from *Aethiopis* (1) and *Sack of Troy* (4). The opening lines of the *Little Iliad* (F 1) might also be thought to imply a treatment of all of the Trojan War, or, at least, more than the usual interpretation of this poem's scope would allow. But the information available suggests that some episodes (in particular the death of Priam: see below, p. 68f.) were treated differently in the *Little Iliad* from their counterparts in the *Sack of Troy*, and this whole approach takes an unnecessarily poor view of Proclus' reliability since by definition it must discount what he says of two separate poets, three separate epics, and the specific number of books in each.

The opening two lines of the poem are preserved as F 1:

> Of Ilium I sing, and of Dardania, land of fine horses, for whose sake the Danaans, servants of Ares, endured many sufferings.

In traditional epic style the subject-matter of the poem is placed as the first word (like the *Iliad*'s 'anger' and the *Odyssey*'s 'man': but this epic's subject-matter is thereby announced as more conventional and predictable than either of Homer's works). Then we have the subject-matter extended by a relative clause (as with the *Iliad's* 'anger...which caused many deaths' or the *Odyssey's* 'man...who wandered far') and a stress on suffering as the theme of the poem (here, too, Homer's epic proems are comparable). The only signficant formal difference is our poet's use of the first-person verb 'I sing' rather than the Iliadic or Odyssean injunctions 'sing to me, Muse'. This has been taken as a sign of lateness, but since Homer means to ask the Muse to sing through him, and the picture of the poet as the Muse's spokesman is widespread in early Greek literature, there is less difference between the two modes of opening than there might at first seem.

The first event of which the *Little Iliad* sang was, according to Proclus, the judgement over Achilles' arms, and then Odysseus' victory (thanks to advice given by Athena) and the consequent madness of Ajax. It may of course be that Proclus has tailored the opening of the epic to fit the close he has imposed upon the *Aethiopis*. But a plunge *in medias res* with the quarrel between Ajax and Odysseus would have been proper for epic.

F 2 elaborates our picture of the judgement of the arms by stating that Nestor advised the Greeks to send scouts under the walls of Troy to eavesdrop on conversation concerning the respective bravery of Ajax and Odysseus. The spies thus sent overhear two young girls disagreeing about precisely this topic. One advances Ajax's claims and says:

'<Ajax is superior,> for Ajax lifted and carried out of the press of war the body of the heroic son of Peleus, while the noble Odysseus was unwilling.'

This seemingly intelligent observation evoked the following crushing rebuke from the other girl:

'What is this you have said? How have you come to speak so contrary to reason? Even a woman could carry such a burden – provided a man were to set it upon her. But she could not fight <in the way Odysseus did, conducting a rear-guard action to cover Ajax's retreat>.'

These words, reported back, will have secured Odysseus' victory. There need be no contradiction between the fragment's reference to Nestor's advice and the naming of Athena as adviser which we find in Proclus. (Nestor may have been inspired by Athena, the scouts may have been directed to the young girls by the goddess and so on.) Such double-motivation is quintessentially epic. Various versions of the judgement of Achilles' armour were current in antiquity (above, p. 57f.). According to the most straightforward, a panel of Greek chieftains decided the issue. But as early as *Od.* 11.547 'the judges were the children of the Trojans, and Pallas Athena'. Some poets (perhaps including the author of the *Aethiopis*) interpreted this paradoxical statement to mean that the opinion of Trojan captives was sought (by a familiar idiom, the phrase 'the children of the Trojans' cited from the *Odyssey* will be a mere periphrasis for 'the Trojans'). But the version adopted by the poet of the *Little Iliad* ingeniously (and also perversely) placed a more literal interpretation on 'children' by having the two Trojan girls (with their implausible knowledge of and interest in military matters) decide the issue. It is hard not to see this as a later elaboration of the more straightforward tradition(s) mentioned above.

Odysseus' victory over Ajax (foreshadowed allusively by Odysseus' defeat of Ajax in the wrestling-match at *Il.* 23.708ff.) drives the latter out of his mind. Such madness is highly unHomeric as we have seen above (p. 42). In this state Ajax slaughtered the cattle of the Achaeans and committed suicide, according to Proclus. Presumably a fuller account of this episode would more or less coincide with the background presupposed in Sophocles' tragedy *Ajax*: The hero had originally planned to murder Agamemnon and Menelaus (an unHomeric act of treachery) and Athena deflects his attention onto the cattle. On becoming sane and recognising what he had done he killed himself (a further unHomeric action). F 3 of the *Little Iliad* observes that Ajax's body was not cremated in the normal heroic way, but buried in a coffin because of Agamemnon's anger <at the way Ajax had tried to murder him>. The motivation here seems to represent a relatively late rationalisation. The original purpose behind the treatment of Ajax's corpse will probably have related to his suicide: the belief that those who have died by their own hands must be buried differently from those who die normally is primitive and world-wide and takes many manifestations.

Proclus' summary proceeds to relate that after this Odysseus captured Helenus in an ambush, and the latter delivered a prophecy concerning the sack of Troy. Diomedes then brought back Philoctetes from Lemnos. We have already had cause to mention the unHomeric figure of Priam's seer-son Helenus in connection with the *Cypria* (above, p. 38). Given that the detail about his prophecy is followed by Diomedes' despatch to Lemnos, it would be simple-minded not to infer a connection between the two. Helenus presumably revealed what we know from later sources – an oracle that Troy could not fall without Philoctetes and his bow. Philoctetes is another unHomeric figure, already encountered in the context of the *Cypria* (above, p. 45). Note too the recurrent stress on the oracular.

What does Proclus tell us next of the *Little Iliad*'s contents? Philoctetes, brought back to Troy, was healed by <Asclepius' son> Machaon and proceeded to kill Paris in a duel. Paris' corpse was mutilated by Menelaus and then the Trojans recovered it and gave it burial. Machaon is a figure whose fate varies wildly according to whatever poet is dealing with him. In some accounts (cf. above, p. 51f.) he was despatched by Penthesileia. In the *Little Iliad* he survives to cure Philoctetes (and then, in F 7, be killed by Eurypylus: see below, p. 65). In yet a third account he is still around to be included among the heroes that lurked within the Trojan Horse.

Menelaus' mutilation of Paris' body is one more of the poem's unHomeric features. Such mutilations are often threatened in the *Iliad* but do not actually occur (with the (partial) exception of Achilles' behaviour towards Hector's corpse). That Menelaus (a notably mild and humane character within the Homeric tradition) should have been portrayed as doing this to his enemy's corpse speaks volumes for the difference in ethos between the *Iliad* and *Odyssey* and a poem like ours.

Paris being dead, the poet of the *Little Iliad* supplied Helen with another spouse: Proclus tells us that Paris' brother Deiphobus married her (cf. *Od.* 4.276).

Next (Proclus continues) Odysseus fetched Neoptolemus from the isle of Scyros and presented him with his father Achilles' armour. How Achilles came to have ever been on Scyros was explained in the *Cypria* (see above, p. 43). It was also touched on in the *Little Iliad*, for F 4[A] of the poem preserves an account of how

> Peleus' son Achilles was brought to Scyros by a gale and there during that night he put in at an unwelcoming harbour.

The Iliadic scholion that quotes these verses gives their context as the storm that scattered the Greek forces after the abortive Teuthranian expedition (above, p. 42). From the same portion of the poem must derive F 5 with its description of the spear once given to Peleus by Chiron (see above, p. 35) and later wielded by Achilles:

> The golden hoop flashes brightly and fastened by it the two-pronged spear...

Since early Greek poetry does not seem to have employed the historic present, the word meaning 'flashes' must either be emended to the past tense (which is easily done) or we must infer that the fragment comes from a direct speech. The late epic poet Quintus of Smyrna (third century AD) included in his *Posthomerica* a scene in which Odysseus described to Neoptolemus, while they were still on Scyros, his father's armour. Perhaps the *Little Iliad* had a similar scene.

We return to Proclus to learn that at Troy Achilles appeared in a vision to his son Neoptolemus (cf. below, p. 78). Then Eurypylus, the son of Telephus, arrived to serve as the Trojans' ally. He performed deeds of valour but was then slain by Neoptolemus. Eurypylus, as we learn from later writers, especially Sophocles' tragedy of that name (*Tr.G.F.* 4.195ff. Radt), was despatched to Troy by his mother, whom Priam bribed to send him (compare the like motif involving Harmonia's necklace within the Theban cycle. F 6 is part of a description of the bribe, which was obviously mentioned in parenthesis. It consisted of a golden vine crafted by Hephaestus:

> The vine which Zeus son of Cronus gave <to Laomedon> as a compensation for <the abduction of> his son <Ganymedes>, a vine flowering with golden leaves †...† and with grape-clusters which Hephaestus had wrought and presented to father Zeus, and he in turn gave it to Laomedon in return for Ganymedes.

The description of an object which has been passed down to man from the gods and then through generations of men is a familiar one in Homeric epic (compare, for instance, Agamemnon's sceptre in *Il.* 2.101ff.). Much less Homeric, however, is the passage's frank avowal of Zeus' homosexual abduction of Ganymedes, an individual mentioned no more than twice in Homer (and then only in the context of the family-tree of the Trojan royal house, never as Zeus' cup-bearer on Olympus, a role reserved for Hebe). Also unHomeric is the notion that a warrior's participation in battle is explicable through motives other than heroism. Eurypylus' death at Neoptolemus' hands is mentioned at *Od.* 11.519ff. and it is no coincidence that Memnon is also named in that passage. For Eurypylus is a doublet of the Aethiopian king, handily providing Achilles' son with a worthy antagonist to kill on the battlefield before Troy is captured. Just as the *Cypria* postponed the Greeks' arrival at Troy with various elaborate retardations (above, p. 42ff.), so the poet of the *Little Iliad* seems to have put off the capture of the city by a number of devices ostensibly working towards that end (Helenus' prophecy, the fetching of Philoctetes and Neoptolemus, Paris' death). But now the very last of Priam's allies has been summoned and despatched, and it is hardly surprising to learn from Proclus' résumé that the next episode involved the besieging of the city by the Greeks.

Its first development (to continue with Proclus' summary) was that, on Athena's suggestion, Epeius devised the trick involving the Trojan Horse. Epeius is one of those heroes who feature in *Iliad* 23's Funeral Games for Patroclus and there attain an eminence that reflects their importance in the Epic Cycle rather than the *Iliad* itself. Indeed, Epeius does not feature in Homer outside that one episode. The building of the Wooden Horse is variously ascribed in ancient writers to Athena, to Epeius, or to Odysseus, most often to Epeius *on the prompting* of Athena or Odysseus. Even at this stage the sack of Troy does not immediately follow on. There were further retardations. Proclus tells us that the next development was for Odysseus to disfigure himself and thus disguised to enter Troy as a spy. Here he was recognised by Helen and conferred with her about the capture of the city. He then killed some Trojans and returned safe to the Greek ships. Some such tradition of Odysseus' infiltration is already presupposed at *Od.* 4.244ff. in Helen's account of events leading up to the sack of Troy. F 8 of the *Little Iliad* has its place in this context: Odysseus was wounded by Thoas when they were going to the Trojan citadel together. Some sort of association between Odysseus and Thoas, leader of the Aetolian contingent against Troy, is implied by another Odyssean passage, the false tale spun by Odysseus at 14.469ff. The last episode related in Apollodorus' *Epitome* involves an unusual tradition that Odysseus was tried before Neoptolemus for his killing of the suitors and, being exiled, went to Aetolia and married Thoas' daughter. The present fragment of our epic belongs to this circle of tales associating the two heroes. Its detail of the wounding does not entail any hostility: on the contrary it shows close co-operation between the pair. As a further means of escaping suspicion, Odysseus had his comrade wound him to increase the verisimilitude of his disguise (compare the tale of the voluntarily mutilated Zopyrus in Herodotus 3.156-8).

After this (to return to Proclus) Odysseus, with Diomedes' aid, carried off the Palladium from Troy. Here too Odysseus' collaboration with a colleague has Homeric precedent (see above, p. 48), but this episode is more profoundly unHomeric in several ways. Firstly the Palladium, a divine talisman on whose preservation in Troy the city's safety depends, is a piece of superstition and folk-lore which Homer

The Little Iliad 67

nowhere sees fit to mention. Further, we gather from F 9 that the *Little Iliad*'s narrative of this episode was connected in antiquity with the proverbial saying 'Diomedes' compulsion'. The only way to make sense of this connection is to suppose that the epic included details about the theft of the Palladium which are only explicitly recorded by later writers: that Odysseus tried to gain sole possession of the talisman by literally stabbing Diomedes in the back; but that Diomedes turned round in time, drew his sword and drove Odysseus before him, beating his back with the flat of his sword. In other words, like the detail of Palamedes' death in the *Cypria* (above, p. 48), another unHomeric story of cowardice, treachery and deceit.

Finally the ruse of the wooden horse was put into effect. Proclus says that the Greeks placed the best of their heroes inside the horse; then the remainder set fire to their huts and sailed off to Tenedos. F 10 of our epic, preserved by Apollodorus, seems to claim that the *Little Iliad* stated that three thousand warriors were lurking inside the horse, but this extravagantly large number cannot be right, even if one accepts that the poet need not have named them all. The warriors hidden inside the horse were in all likelihood originally conceived of as an advance force whose main, indeed only, function was to let in the main body of troops. A small hand-picked body of men would suffice for this and it is easy to correct the number that stands in our text of Apollodorus to something more in line with this concept (e.g. 'thirteen').

Proclus' résumé of the events in the *Little Iliad* ends with a sentence describing the reaction of the Trojans to the Greek ploy. Imagining their misfortunes were at an end, they brought the Trojan Horse into the city, demolishing part of the wall to do so, and then proceeded to feast and celebrate their imagined victory over the Greeks.

At this point, Proclus' summary of the *Little Iliad* is artificially curtailed, for reasons we examined above (p. 60), and a transition to the events described near the beginning of the *Sack of Troy* is contrived. However, we still possess a large number of fragments relating to details covered by that portion of the *Little Iliad* for which we no longer possess Proclus' résumé, and it seems best to consider these next before turning to the separate epic called the *Sack of Troy*.

F 11 touched on the time of night at which the sack of Troy began:

It was the middle of night, and the bright moon was starting to rise.

From the references to midnight and the rising moon later authors tried to calculate the exact month and day of the year when the sack took place.

Fragments 12-18 and 21-3 of the *Little Iliad* all derive from the description of the famous painting of the Sack of Troy by Polygnotus which the second-century AD writer Pausanias gives in Book 10 of his *Periegesis* or Guide to Greece. Several details in this visual representation are compared or contrasted with the traditions followed in our epic. Thus in F 12 Pausanias says that Lesches in his poem (see above, p. 60) described the wounding of the Greek warrior Meges in the arm by Admetus son of Augeas, and of the Greek Lycomedes in the wrist by Agenor, and that Polygnotus derived his depiction of those wounds from the epic. In F 13 we learn of another epic account of wounding, this time of the Trojan Helicaon: he was then recognised by Odysseus and led out of the battle. This detail is to be explained in the light of the tradition found in *Il.* 3.123f. and 205ff. that when Menelaus and Odysseus visited Troy on their embassy for the recovery of Helen (above, p. 46) they were entertained by Antenor, Helicaon's father. Hence Odysseus' present act of friendship and gratitude. F 14, describing Polygnotus' portrayal of Neoptolemus smiting the Trojan Astynous, informs us that Astynous was mentioned in our epic. F 15 is a short list of other slayings: the poem had the Trojan Eioneus killed by Neoptolemus and Admetus (mentioned also in F 12) by Philoctetes. F 16 is another such detail: Coroebus, the fiancé of Cassandra, was killed in our epic by Diomedes, though the majority of authors name Neoptolemus in this role. F 17 touches on what must have been the climactic death in the sack of Troy, that of Priam: unlike other accounts, our epic did not have the old king despatched at the altar of Zeus *Herkeios*, Zeus god of the hearth (see below, p. 72). Rather, Neoptolemus dragged him from the altar and finished him off at the doors of his own palace. F 18 deals with an incidental death, that of Axion, one of the remaining sons of Priam, who was killed by Eurypylus son of Euaemon. Agenor, the fragment adds, was killed by Neoptolemus (for Agenor see also F 12). F 21 (from the same portion of Pausanias' account of Polygnotus' painting) deals with the Trojan women taken captive after the sack: Andromache's son <Astyanax>, we are told, was thrown to his death from a tower and this was due not to a formal decision of the Greeks but to Neoptolemus acting on a purely personal grudge. Finally, F 23 deals with the fate of Aethra, mother of the great Athenian hero Theseus, whose presence at Troy was explained in the cyclic epic, the *Sack of Troy* (see below, p. 75). She had been one of Helen's handmaids but was now recognised by her grandsons Demophon <and Acamas>, and the former asked Agamemnon that she be restored to them. This he did, after first ascertaining that Helen had no objections. Leaving aside for the moment Aethra herself, we may still find this episode very unHomeric, because the sons of Theseus feature in neither the *Iliad* nor the *Odyssey*: the former epic, indeed, depicts the leader of the Athenian forces at Troy as Menestheus, a remarkably colourless and unmemorable figure of whom little is heard outside the pages of that epic. And it gave much trouble to later writers and mythographers to explain just why in the *Iliad* it is this nonentity, rather than the expected sons of Theseus, who appears as the Athenian commander.

Two more fragments, not preserved by Pausanias, contain further details of events in the sack of Troy as described by the *Little Iliad*. F 19 deals with the encounter between Menelaus and Helen: the angry husband drew his sword to punish the erring wife, but the weapon fell from his hands at the sight of her breasts. This was a familiar scene in later literature (e.g. Ibycus fr. 296P and Euripides *Andr*. 629ff.) and art. Its eroticism goes beyond anything Homer allows himself, even in his relatively chaste and restrained accounts of lovemaking. The meeting between Hector and Andromache at the end of *Iliad* 6 nobly depicts the tenderness of married love, but its physical expression goes no further than the holding of hands and touching, and when Hector turns to leave it is his son Astyanax not Andromache that he kisses and fondles.

This aptly brings us to the longest extant fragment of the *Little Iliad*, the account of the death of Astyanax in F 20:

> But the glorious son of great-hearted Achilles arranged for
> Hector's wife to be sent off down to the hollow ships. And

> taking the child from the bosom of his fair-tressed nurse he whirled him around by the foot and then cast him from the top of the tower. He fell and then dark death and mighty fate seized upon him.
>
> And he selected for himself Andromache, the fair-girdled spouse of Hector, whom, in fact, the leaders of the assembled Achaean force had given him to keep as a pleasing prize, thus requiting him; and also the noble offspring of Anchises, tamer of horses, Aeneas, he caused to set foot on the sea-faring ships to lead him off as a choice prize over and above those of the other Danaans, surpassing them all.

One of the great insoluble mysteries associated with the Epic Cycle is that the second paragraph here is attributed by a different quoter to the Hellenistic poet Simias. Even if we confine our attentions to the first paragraph, as alone unambiguously attributed to the *Little Iliad*, we cannot fail to register a sense of disappointment. The death of the infant Astyanax, which might have been anticipated as a moment of high pathos and tragedy, is described (as numerous scholars have complained) in a dry, dull manner, as if it were a sack of potatoes, rather than a human being, that was being dumped over the walls. In comparison with the moving *anticipation* of the same event by Hector in *Il.* 6.447ff., the *Little Iliad's* passage does not exist as poetry. But this is ever the way of the world: a great poet like Homer can foreshadow an event more poignantly than a second-rate poet (like the *Little Iliad's*) can actually describe it.

9: The Sack of Troy

Proclus' summary opens with the Trojans suspicious and debating what to do with the horse: some were for pitching it off a high peak, some for burning it, some for dedicating it as sacred to Athena. The last-mentioned opinion prevailed. There is some inconcinnity here with the close of the *Little Iliad*'s summmary, which left the Trojans innocently rejoicing at the termination of the war. There is also a contradiction arising if we try to treat the two résumés as providing a seamless narrative: it is odd of the Trojans first to demolish part of their city wall to let the horse in and only then deliberate whether to preserve it or not. One infers two original traditions: deliberation outside the walls followed by demolition, or deliberation inside with no preceding demolition. Next, we are told, the Trojans turned to rejoicing and feasting, since they were quit of the war (Proclus' language here closely echoes that in the last sentence of his résumé of the *Little Iliad*: it is odd that this duplication was not avoided.

The next episode concerns the fate of Laocoon and his sons. Two snakes appeared and killed him and one of his children. Alarmed at this omen Aeneas and his men secretly left the city and betook themselves to Mt. Ida. This is our earliest extant literary reference to the role of Laocoon in the sack of Troy: he is a figure very important for later authors (especially Sophocles in his lost play of that name: see *Tr.G.F.* 4.330ff. Radt) but manifestly conspicuous by his absence from Homer. These later sources specify the elder of the two sons as the snakes' other victim. If the same tradition occurred in our epic, the portent to which Aeneas and his followers react might be thus interpreted: the two snakes are Agamemnon and Menelaus; Laocoon the father symbolises the doomed city of Troy, and the elder son represents the death of Priam, eldest son of Laomedon. The survival of the younger son is an allusion to the survival of Aeneas. Whatever the precise details, the prophetic function of the event would be alien to Homer. But this reconstruction is extremely hypothetical; better to remind ourselves that we have no idea why, in the Sack of Troy's scheme of things, Laocoon suffers as he does and whether (as in some later accounts) Apollo is to be envisaged as punishing his priest by sending the snakes. We can, however, at least infer that this epic envisaged Aeneas and his descendants as remaining in the Troad (a tradition also implied by such early sources as Il. 20.307f., H.H. Aphr. 196 and 256ff., Hes. Th. 1010).

The details that Proclus proceeds to recount are familiar from later authors, in particular the account of Troy's sack that occurs in Book Two of Vergil's *Aeneid*. Sinon sent a fire-signal to the Greeks, having first entered the city in disguise (cf. *Aen*. 2.57ff.). The Greeks then sail off from Tenedos (see above, p. 67) while the heroes hidden within the horse issued forth and fell upon the enemy, and, having killed many of them, captured the city by force. Neoptolemus killed king Priam at the altar of Zeus god of the hearth to which the old man had fled for safety (for the *Little Iliad*'s different tradition see above, p. 68). Menelaus came across Helen and led her off to the ships having killed Deiphobus (see above, pp. 64 and 69).

The next major section of the poem dealt with Locrian Ajax's assault on Cassandra, daughter of Priam. She had taken refuge at the temple of Athena and was clinging to the goddess' wooden image when Ajax dragged her off with such force that the image came away too. The Greeks were appalled at this act of desecration and planned to stone Ajax, but he took refuge at the altar of Athena and was thus saved. This story of the crime and punishment of Locrian Ajax gets no mention in Homer (though Il. 23.773ff. may imply some hostility between this hero and Athena) but it was popular in later writers (e.g. Sophocles' lost *Ajax the Locrian*: see *Tr.G.F.* 4.102ff. Radt). We must be careful to segregate the early epic account from some of the later treatments (e.g. the notion that Ajax actually raped Cassandra in front of Athena's statue, which averted its eyes from the sacrilege, need not predate Callimachus fr. 35 Pf). Later writers mention an oath made by Ajax (its content is uncertain) and trial by the Greeks, and some scholars have combined the two details and placed them after the flight to Athena's altar. However, a closer examination of the evidence would suggest that the oath was made at a relatively early stage just after the initial act of desecration. Cassandra was removed from Ajax and given as booty to Agamemnon (see below, p. 80). According to Apollod. *Epit.* 5.23, when the Greeks were on the point of sailing off, they were checked by Calchas who warned them of Athena's anger over the impiety of Ajax. The Greeks were ready to kill him but he escaped to the altar and they left him there. This may have been the course of events in the Epic Cycle. Whatever its content, Ajax's oath failed to appease Athena; on Calchas' advice the Greeks tried Ajax and were prepared to avert their communal guilt by stoning the guilty man. He, however, broke loose and fled to the altar of Athena. By this action he doubled his guilt and by failing to take the matter further the Greeks too incurred further guilt.

The next words of Proclus' summary specify the form taken by the goddess' punishment. The Greeks, it is said, sailed off and Athena plotted destruction for them on the high sea. And yet the remainder of Proclus' résumé deals with events that took place while the Greeks had not yet left Troy, and his summary of the *Returns Home* begins with the Greeks still at the city. Numerous attempts have been made to remove this contradiction. The simplest and most convincing supposes that the *Sack of Troy* originally looked forward to the wreck of the Greek fleet consequent upon Ajax's crime. This sequel has somehow got incorporated into Proclus' résumé as if it were part of the actual narrative (and the corresponding section in the *Returns*' narrative has been eliminated as a doublet. We are finally told of the sacrifice of Polyxena on Achilles' tomb (see above, p. 49f.), Odysseus' killing of Astyanax, and Andromache's distribution to Neoptolemus (cf. above, p. 69f.).

Such is Proclus' summary of the epic's contents. Now let us consider the handful of actual fragments we possess. The longest and most interesting deals with an episode that probably fell outside the strict confines of the poem and featured parenthetically. This is the madness of Telamonian Ajax (F 1):

> For their father <Poseidon> † the earth-shaker...† had given them both <skill in medicine> and had made each more glorious than the other. On the one he bestowed nimbler hands and the power to cut darts from the flesh and heal all wounds, and in the other he set in his chest all means of unerring discernment both to recognise the unknowable and to cure the incurable. This latter

son it was, in fact, who was the first to detect the mad anger of
Ajax, both his flashing eyes and his burdened mind.

These lines are deeply unHomeric in several ways. Firstly, the distinction between chirurgy as practised by Machaon and the diagnostic skill of Podalirius – who is able thereby to infer the madness of Ajax – is a refinement not specifically present in the *Iliad* or *Odyssey*. Next, the very notion of insanity (as opposed to e.g. heroic wrath or battle-frenzy) is largely avoided in the Homeric epics (see pp. 42 and 62). From the wording of our fragment it would be both difficult and dangerous to conclude how strictly the poet ever distinguished between genuine lunacy and the sense of heroic aggrievement at failure to win Achilles' armour which may have been the starting-point of that madness. But no special skills would be required to detect normal heroic resentment. Finally Machaon and Podalirius feature in Homer as the sons of Asclepius, the physician-god. In the *Sack of Troy*, however, they are (rather unusually) regarded as the offspring of Poseidon. There is some, admittedly tenuous, evidence that this god was worshipped on the island of Tenedos under the title *iatros* or 'healer', and *Od.* 9.520f., where Polyphemus unconvincingly tells Odysseus that his father Poseidon will cure his blinded eye, has also been associated with our fragment.

F 2 was only re-discovered at a relatively recent date (about thirty years ago) when the elimination of a mere single letter from a hitherto unintelligible word revealed 'Arctinus' as the source of the remarkable notion that the eyes, tail (and knees) of the Trojan Horse were capable of movement. The scholar responsible for this emendation compared Hephaestus' mobile automata in *Il.* 18.417ff., but the world of Olympus is surely different from that of mankind, and a more apt observation would be that we now have yet one more instance of the Epic Cycle's predilection for the fantastic, the miraculous and the picturesque. Athena's involvement in the construction of the Horse (see above, p. 66) may partly explain the concept (and the horse's alleged size: 50 x 100 feet).

F 3 deals with the throwing of Astyanax from the walls of Troy, a detail that also had its place in the *Little Iliad* (above, p. 69f.).

F 4 alludes to Acamas and Demophon, the sons of Theseus who led the Athenian contingent to Troy (another detail shared with the *Little Iliad*: see above, p.69). According to one unspecified strand of tradition,

The Sack of Troy 75

all they received by way of booty was their grandmother Aethra who had been brought to Troy together with other of Helen's possessions, having originally been carried off from Athens when the Dioscuri brought back Helen from Theseus' clutches (above, p. 39). The author of the *Sack of Troy*, we are told, was more generous, or at least represented Agamemnon as so being:

> And on the sons of Theseus lord Agamemnon bestowed gifts, as he did also on Menestheus, great-hearted shepherd of his people.

It has been suggested that the gifts in question were the portions of land in the vicinity of Troy which we find mentioned at Aesch. *Eum.* 397ff. and Eur. *Tro.* 30ff. It is anyway clear that the *Sack of Troy* combined the Homeric tradition, whereby the otherwise obscure Menestheus was the Athenian commander (see above, p. 69), with the more familiar and intelligible version that the sons of Theseus occupied this role.

A final fragment would cast fascinating light on our epic if only we could be sure that it genuinely preserves matter deriving from it (*fr. dub.*). This long passage from the historian Dionysius of Halicarnassus (whose *floruit* is 30 BC) professes to give the early history of the Trojan Palladium (above, p. 66f.) from the time when, together with other items of dowry deriving from Athena, it came into the possession of Dardanus, who later founded Troy. An oracle relating to the Palladium is cited:

> In the city which you found, dedicate it to the gods as a permanent object of reverence and reverence it with protective watches and sacrifices and dances. For, as long as these gifts of <Athena> the daughter of Zeus to your wife, venerable as they are, remain in your land, so long will your city be unsacked for all its day forever.

Doubts as to which (if any) of these details come from the *Sack of Troy*, doubts in particular as to whether the oracle is quoted from there, begin to obtrude when, towards the end of his account, Dionysius states that Aeneas escaped with the surviving Palladium, since Odysseus and Diomedes had previously purloined the other one, and that Aeneas brought his Palladium to Italy. Arctinus (Dionysius continues) says that one Palladium was given to Dardanus by Zeus and remained hidden until the city's sack, whereas a mere replica placed on open display was what the Greeks had stolen. This sophisticated (and sophistical) account has a very late ring to it, since such a distinction would otherwise be dated to a time when the development of the Aeneas-legend in Rome made it imperative to have that hero convey Palladium and Penates from Troy to Rome. The account is further flawed by an internal contradiction, since Troy falls though the Palladium is still within Troy.

10: The Returns Home

The epic is by Agias and comprised five books. At the start of Proclus' résumé we read that Athena caused a quarrel to break out between the two brothers Menelaus and Agamemnon over the question of sailing off from Troy. The tradition of this quarrel also occurs in *Od.* 3.135ff. where we are told that Menelaus was for sailing home straight away, while Agamemnon wished to keep the army back and appease Athena by a sacrifice of hecatombs. The hostility of this goddess (which underlies both accounts) is to be explained, of course, in terms of Ajax's earlier crimes (above, p. 72f.). A dispute between heroes is a standard motif of epic (see p. 45). Consistently with the background implied by the Odyssean lines, Proclus' summary next portrays Agamemnon as staying behind at Troy in an attempt to abate the anger of Athena. Diomedes and Nestor, in contrast, sailed off and were the only portion of the expedition to reach home safely. This is the picture consistently presented by all our sources, though some variously specify troubles awaiting Diomedes on his return home, and a number of scholars would trace at least some of these traditions back to our epic.

It is again consistent with the Odyssean schema that Proclus' résumé should next report how Menelaus sailed forth after Diomedes and Nestor had left, and finally reached Egypt with five ships, the remainder having been destroyed by storm at sea. Consistent both with the passage about the Atreidae's quarrel cited above, and with Menelaus' presence in Egypt as related in his speech to Telemachus at *Od.* 4.351ff.

According to the next section of Proclus' résumé, Calchas, Leontes and Polypoetes went on foot to Colophon and there buried Tiresias, who had died. Here we finally move into a relatively unHomeric section of the poem, though the three Greek leaders are all mentioned in the *Iliad*. Apollod. *Epit.* 6.2 has a slightly fuller account of this episode whereby Amphilochus (brother of Alcmaeon (see pp. 27 and 29)) and Podalirius (see p. 74) are also among the Greek leaders, and it is not Tiresias but

Calchas who is buried. Calchas' death is then explained: it was foretold to him that he would die on meeting a prophet more skilled than himself and it so happened that the Greek leaders lodged with Mopsus, a prophet who fitted the bill and displayed his superiority. Even before the publication of Apollodorus' *Epitome* (see p. 6f.) some scholars had wanted to emend the name of Tiresias in Proclus' résumé to that of Calchas. The relevance of Tiresias, who should have died some time in the past, is by no means immediately clear. But Tiresias' daughter Manto is connected with Colophon (see above, p. 30), and the Greek leaders may have erected a cenotaph or memorial to Tiresias rather than actually burying him. Besides, we know that the *Returns Home* included a visit to the Underworld and this may have somehow related to the present mention of the Theban seer. Calchas' presence among the chieftains was presumably significant in another way: knowing (cf. above, p. 73) the dangers posed by Athena's anger he presumably persuaded his comrades that it was safer to travel by land.

Proclus' summary now returns to Agamemnon's forces at Troy. Perhaps it here preserves the structure of the original epic which, following the Homeric practice of narrating simultaneous events consecutively, may have first busied itself with the fortunes of those who sailed off (or marched off by land) first, and then related the fates of the warriors who, like Agamemnon, delayed their departure. We are told that, as Agamemnon and his troops sailed off, the ghost of Achilles appeared and tried to detain them by warnings of what was going to happen. Whether these warnings were confined to Agamemnon's murder or also embraced Ajax's drowning we cannot be sure; we may at least observe that once again a poem from the Epic Cycle displays an unHomeric fondness for prophetic or oracular hints at the future course of events (cf. above, pp. 38f., 45).

Next in Proclus' résumé comes the storm at sea in the vicinity of the Capherian rocks, and Ajax's destruction. Caphereus is on the southern promontory of Euboea. *Od.* 4.500f., by contrast, places the death of Ajax near the Gyraean rocks, off the islands of Mykonos, Delos and Tenos, and other later accounts have other locations. Later writers (beginning with Eur. *Tro.* 75ff.) depict Athena as despatching the impious Ajax with her father Zeus' thunderbolt. Such a detail is missing from the account of Ajax's death given in *Od.* 4.499ff. and seems, in fact, intensely unHomeric (compare the remarks above on the traditional account of the impious Capaneus' obliteration before Thebes (p. 26)) but it may have originated with our epic.

A new episode of the *Returns Home* began, as Proclus informs us, with Neoptolemus, on his grandmother Thetis' advice, making the journey home by foot. He thereby avoided the consequences of Athena's anger, like Calchas and the other chieftains mentioned earlier. He came to Thrace and there encountered Odysseus at the town of Maroneia (not mentioned in the *Odyssey*, though later writers identified it with that epic's Ismarus). Apollod. *Epit.* 6.5 adds the detail that, before setting out, Neoptolemus remained on Tenedos for two days. Some scholars have combined this with the tradition preserved in *Od.* 3.130ff. and 11.533ff. to produce a version wherein Neoptolemus leaves Troy together with the fleets of Diomedes, Nestor and Odysseus, but after the quarrel there mentioned and Odysseus' return to Agamemnon, hesitates at Tenedos before receiving Thetis' advice.

According to Proclus, Neoptolemus, after the meeting with Odysseus, finished the rest of his journey and buried Phoenix, who had died. He then came to the land of the Molossians and made himself known to his grandfather Peleus. All this is practically identical to the account in Apollodorus as cited above, save that this adds that Helenus (see above, p. 63) was in Neoptolemus' company at the time, and says nothing of an encounter with Peleus.

The final sentence of Proclus' summary is perhaps the part that has most interested scholars, the part we would most like to see expanded. It begins with the return home of Agamemnon: he was killed by Aegisthus and Clytemnestra, and avenged by Orestes and Pylades. Unfortunately for those interested in the pre-Aeschylean history of the story of the house of Atreus, this account is far too concentrated and elliptical. We should like to know much more about (for instance) the role of Aegisthus (does his mention before Clytemnestra imply he took the leading role in Agamemnon's murder?) and of Pylades (whose name is conspicuous by its absence from the Odyssean account (3.305ff.) of Orestes' revenge, as it is, indeed, from the *Odyssey* as a whole). If the 'Homeric Cup' (T 2) of Hellenistic workmanship and date really does, as its incomplete inscription suggests, portray the death of Agamemnon as described in our epic, that death was presented in Odyssean terms. For the cup shows Clytemnestra attacking Agamemnon with a sword over the corpse of Cassandra, and the setting is clearly a banquet (cf. *Od.* 11.405ff.). But Cassandra's absence from Proclus' summary at this point is a further reminder of how inadequate our knowledge of this crucial episode in the *Returns Home* is.

The very last item in Proclus' summary (and perhaps in the poem too) is the safe arrival home of Menelaus, a detail about which we know and care less.

So much for Proclus' summary. What of our actual fragments?

F 1 reminds us a little of *Cypria* F 18 in the etymological appropriateness of the names involved: Nauplius is father of Palamedes, Oeax and Nausimedon: the first and fourth names are redolent of ships while the third literally signifies a part of a ship (the handle of the rudder). There is no evidence that (as is often supposed) the *Returns Home* necessarily included the unHomeric story that Nauplius, to avenge the death of his son Palamedes (see above, p. 48), lit false beacons that lured many of the homeward bound Greek ships on to hidden rocks. It is not difficult to imagine a number of other contexts for this fragment's family tree.

F 2 is further evidence of a tendency within the Epic Cycle which we have already considered (above, p. 38f. etc.): the proliferation of children and the fleshing-out of minor characters mentioned in passing by Homer. In this particular case the name of the slave girl who is said in *Od.* 4.12 to have borne Megapenthes to Menelaus is specified as Getis.

The existence of some sort of *Nekyia* or visit to the Underworld (as in *Odyssey* 11), though such an episode goes unmentioned in Proclus' sparse summary, seems indicated by the next three fragments. They all derive from Pausanias' description of the painting of the Odyssean *Nekyia* by Polygnotus (see above, p. 68). F 3 is largely concerned to convey negative information – that our poem did not mention the demonic spirit Eurynomus who eats away the flesh of the dead. But in passing it establishes that this epic did contain an account of the fearful scenes in the Underworld where such a detail might have been expected (perhaps we should contrast this with the remarkably rational and unfrightening depiction of the Underworld which we receive from the *Odyssey*'s eleventh book). F 4 presents us with another family tree: the *Returns Home* made Clymene daughter of Minyas and wife of Cephalus, to whom she bore Iphiclus. F 5 likewise tells us that Maera was daughter of Proetus son of Thersander, son of Sisyphus; and that she died while still a young, unmarried girl.

The three lines of our epic preserved as F 6 constitute the longest direct quotation from the work. That may not seem very impressive, but in fact they supply a very interesting picture. The subject-matter is Medea's rejuvenation of Jason's aged father Aeson:

> Straightaway she made Aeson a dear youthful boy by scraping away his old age in her cunning wisdom, as she boiled many herbs in her golden cauldron.

These verses will not satisfy seekers after a beautiful (or even a bearable) poetic style. Although the fragment is relatively short, it contains a number of infelicities of expression such as we have come to expect from the Epic Cycle, in particular the awkward reference to Aeson as a dear youthful boy, which is probably to be explained as a clumsy adaptation of a passage in *Il*. 9.444ff. where similar language is used. But the contents are important. As usual we may start by observing how unHomeric they are. The Iliadic lines just referred to come from a speech by Phoenix deploring his old age and toying with the notion that a god might scrape it from him and restore his youth. What in Homer is a pathetic, unrealisable fantasy becomes reality in the *Returns Home*. The addiction to the magical and the miraculous is characteristic. A widespread and primitive belief that boiling in a magic cauldron ('The Cauldron of Immortality') can rejuvenate underlies the fragment; the depiction of old age as an almost physical entity requiring to be 'scraped away' recurs not only in *Iliad* 9 but in the *Homeric Hymn* to Aphrodite (v.224) and is again a very primitive motif.

How Medea and her magic cauldron ever came to be mentioned in our poem it is not easy to see.

F 7 is less revealing still:

> Gifts often deceive the minds and deeds of men

is the generalisation seemingly preserved in it. But the single line thus constituted has been deemed seriously corrupt (textually speaking) and the very attribution to our poem depends on an emendation (the manuscripts of the author who quotes the line attribute it to 'Augias' who has to be corrected to '(H)agias' (see p. 77) if the line is to be secured for our epic).

A more important issue is raised by two passages in the second-century AD writer Athenaeus (see above, p. 1) which refer to the *Return Home of the Sons of Atreus*. In theory this might be a further epic on a similar theme to that of the *Returns Home*. Most scholars, however, have preferred to suppose that it is an alternative title for that epic or refers to a portion (the concluding portion?: see p. 79f.) of that epic. F 8 ('from the third book') is not very enlightening:

> And Hermiones, dashing in pursuit of Isus on his swift feet,
> struck the muscles of the man's loins with his spear...

F 9, though it does not preserve a direct quotation, is more informative and more interesting. It deals with that famous figure of myth, Tantalus, whose career of crime and its subsequent punishment was variously treated in ancient literature. Our epic would seem to have stressed hedonistic aspects: he was allowed the privilege of dwelling with the gods and Zeus granted him whatever wishes he desired. Tantalus exhibited his insatiable appetite by demanding the same life-style as the gods. An indignant Zeus responds by suspending a stone over the head of Tantalus: he has before him, indeed, all the pleasures of divine existence, but these are spoiled by the ever-present threat of the stone which may fall at any minute.

This episode combines two familiar patterns of story-telling: the rash promise which cannot be reversed, despite its bad consequences (so, on another occasion, Zeus made a similar promise to Semele which led to her destruction); and the seemingly wonderful state of existence which is ruined by a fatal flaw (one thinks of Tithonus, given immortality, but without perpetual youth: see p. 53). The threatening stone in Tantalus' story was compared in antiquity to the similar function occupied by the sword of Damocles. How it came to be mentioned in the *Returns Home* is again rather mysterious. We recall that a visit to the Underworld seems to have featured in our epic: but while Tantalus belongs there in *Od.* 11.582ff., the logic of the story as told in the *Returns* surely presupposes that Tantalus remains with the gods, unable to enjoy the delights of their existence. We may at least observe once more the very unHomeric nature of the tale: Tantalus' easy passage over the gap separating gods from mortals would be unthinkable in the *Iliad* (where the gap is crucial to the meaning of the poem) and hardly more acceptable in the *Odyssey*.

11: The Telegony

The final poem in the Epic Cycle was the *Telegony*, in two books, generally ascribed to Eugammon of Cyrene. For information as to its contents we are almost totally dependent upon Proclus' résumé (the two fragments available are concerned with very small points of detail). However, several scholars believe that we may glean more details about it by examining problematic passages in the *Odyssey* (especially the *Nekyia* or Odysseus' visit to the Underworld in Book Eleven; and the so-called 'Continuation', that is, everything from *Od.* 23.297 down to the end, a large section which many critics regard as a later addition to the poem). After all, the *Telegony* was intended as, in some sense, a sequel to the *Odyssey*; and the scholars alluded to believe that the latter epic, in the form in which we now know it, has been altered by the importation of motifs and details borrowed from the former, perhaps to make it more independent and dispense with any need for a sequel.

It must be said with emphasis that most of the arguments adduced in favour of this hypothesis are extremely speculative, and often rest upon discrepancies in the problematic Odyssean passages which many will think too small to require so elaborate an hypothesis. For instance, some scholars have been surprised at the way in which the aggrieved relatives of the suitors whom Odysseus has murdered, automatically know (in *Od.* 24.490ff.) that Odysseus will be found at his father's farm. And they solve the alleged problem by supposing that the episode is modelled on a similar scene from the *Telegony* were the relatives come to Odysseus' palace because (much more logically) they expect to find him there. But why not allow the poet of *Od.* 24 to exploit the familiar economic assumption that characters know what his audience knows? Or again, the interpretation in question may be thought to raise more problems than it solves. For instance, it has been argued that when Odysseus' mother at *Od.* 11.223f. tells her son to hurry back from Hades to the light of day (which he doesn't) to tell all she has said to him to Penelope (which he doesn't), the scene is modelled on a like one in the lost *Telegony*, in which Odysseus' need to visit the land of the Thesprotians (see below, p. 87) was explained by a visit to the Underworld. But that epic's visit to the Underworld will have required a different motivation from the *Odyssey*'s and it is not easy to supply such a motivation. It is a further obstacle that Proclus' summary says nothing of such a visit to the Underworld, or of other interesting episodes which this line of approach would include in the *Telegony* (e.g. the 'Second Nekyia' at *Od*. 24.1ff., or Odysseus' exile as punishment for killing the suitors, a punishment agreed after the arbitration of Athena). When the incompleteness of Proclus' résumé of other poems in the Epic Cycle has been taken fully into account, it is still disturbing to have to cope with so many additional details.

A further difficulty involves the *Thesprotis* mentioned by Pausanias 8.12.5f. Is this the same epic as the *Telegony* but with an alternative title, a part or portion of the *Telegony* with a separate title, or (as some scholars once believed) an original epic which was later used as source for the *Telegony*? It is impossible to say for certain.

The very first sentence of Proclus' résumé indicates that the *Telegony* was intended to follow on from an *Odyssey* lacking the 'Continuation'. For it tells us that the suitors were buried by their relatives. And yet such a detail is already present in the 'Continuation' (*Od*. 24.417ff.) and the *Telegony* would hardly wish to repeat the motif. There is no difficulty about the next detail: Odysseus sacrificed to the Nymphs. This represents the fulfilment of a pledge uttered by the hero at *Od*. 13.353ff. when he sets foot on his native land for the first time since leaving for Troy.

Next, Odysseus sailed off to Elis in order to look at the oxen-stable there. The likeliest interpretation of this detail does not infer that Odysseus himself owned herds of cattle on the mainland (*Od*. 4.634ff. and 14.100 are irrelevant to this proposition; *Il*. 2.635 perhaps relevant but certainly problematic). Rather, Odysseus was presented in the *Telegony* as visiting the famous cattle-sheds of Augeas king of Elis, well-known as the object of one of Heracles' labours (he had to cleanse them of the accumulated dirt of twenty years). Polyxenus, with whom Odysseus stays, is the grandson of Augeas, who himself features in the inset story soon to be told (see below), so such an interpretation is self-consistent; and the opportunity for the inclusion of such a story was an adequate motive for introducing the trip to Elis.

As indicated above, Proclus' summary proceeds with the statement that Odysseus was entertained by Polyxenus and received as a token of friendship a wine bowl (on which was depicted the tale of Trophonius, Agamedes and Augeas). Polyxenus is a very minor character indeed, mentioned in the Iliadic Catalogue of Ships (*Il.* 2.623f.) and, by virtue of not appearing in that epic's lists of slain, handily available to play the sort of role he does here play at this late stage in the story of Troy. His name, etymologically indicative of hospitality, may have inspired his function here. The expansion of a secondary figure from Homer is thoroughly typical of the Epic Cycle (see above, p. 80 etc.). The whole episode seems to have exploited two familiar motifs of early poetry: the gift of friendship and the *ecphrasis* or description at length of some artefact's contents (compare, for instance, the Shield of Achilles at *Il.* 18.478ff.).

The tale of Trophonius, Agamedes and Augeas is preserved in several later authors: most fully by Charax of Pergamon (*F.Gr.Hist.* 103 F 5) whose retelling, however, perhaps contains late and rationalising elements. Safer, then, to use Pausanias 9.37.5ff. which may well be closer to the *Telegony*'s account: the brothers Trophonius and Agamedes built the temple of Delphi and the treasure-house of Hyrieus (king of the Euboean city of Hyria). But they continually plundered the latter's contents until Hyrieus devised a snare in which, during one expedition of theft, Agamedes became irretrievably caught. To prevent his brother blabbing under torture, Trophonius cut off his head and was then himself swallowed up by the earth in the sacred wood at Lebadeia.

The motif of the treasure-house which is opened secretly and requires human sacrifice underlies this story and is very primitive. More to the point, the story as a whole is strongly reminiscent of the adventures of Rhampsinitus as recounted by Herodotus in Book 2.121 of his Histories. Herodotus attributes this to Egyptian sources, and since the poet to whom the *Telegony* is usually assigned was Eugammon of Cyrene it is hardly surprising that scholars have excitedly inferred that an original Egyptian tale got into the hands of Greek colonists at Cyrene and was thence reworked into the epic known as the *Telegony*. A cooler assessment by Herodotean scholars of recent times would reverse this alleged process: Herodotus himself invented the story of Rhampsinitus, basing it on the *ecphrasis* in the *Telegony*. We need not worry our heads as to that issue. What is striking is the apparently ornamental nature of the *Telegony*'s inset story, which has no obvious thematic relevance to the poem as a whole (compare above, p. 41, on the myths adduced by Nestor in the *Cypria*).

According to our only text of Proclus' résumé, Odysseus then sailed back to Ithaca and performed the sacrifices enjoined by Tiresias <in the Odyssean *Nekyia*>. He then came to the land of the Thesprotians. Two sets of sacrifices are actually specified for Odysseus in the *Odyssey*. Circe bids him slaughter a cow and (in honour of Tiresias) a black sheep (*Od.* 10.522ff. and 11.30ff.); Tiresias bids him slaughter a ram, a bull and a boar to appease Poseidon: this he is to do when he comes to a land so ignorant of sea-faring that the oar he is carrying will be mistaken for a winnowing-fan (*Od.* 11.121ff.). Given the *Telegony*'s general relationship to the *Odyssey* (above, p. 84), the omission of any reference to Circe's orders and their fulfilment would be odd: perhaps Proclus' summary has omitted them from the original account. Apollodorus' *Epitome* (7.34) informs us that, after making himself known to wife and father, Odysseus sacrificed to Hades, Persephone and Tiresias, and then travelled on foot through Epirus to the land of the Thesprotians, where he appeased Poseidon in the manner laid down by Tiresias. It may, therefore, be advisable to emend Proclus' statement that Odysseus sailed to *Ithaca* in a way that produces the sense that he sailed to *Epirus*. This would bring the accounts of Apollodorus and Proclus practically into agreement (the latter's apparent placing of the sacrifice in question *before* Odysseus' arrival in the land of the Thesprotians will be no more than a small clumsiness of expression). It would also eliminate a singularly pointless and unmotivated return to Ithaca from which Odysseus at once sets out again. A small loose end is that at *Od.* 11.132ff. Tiresias mentions a further sacrifice 'to all the other gods' which Odysseus is to make on returning home from the country of the land-lubbers. There is no mention of this in Apollodorus' *Epitome*, nor is it really conceivable in Proclus' summary, where Odysseus remains in the land of the

Thesprotians (unless his final return home to Ithaca is to be thus explained).

Proclus tells us that on arriving in the land of the Thesprotians Odysseus married Callidice their queen. His irresponsibility in so doing while Penelope is still alive has scandalised most scholars, who indignantly contrast the Odyssean hero's behaviour, staying with Calypso only under duress and renouncing both her and Circe for a final reunion with his wife. It may just be worth mentioning, in partial mitigation, that the *Telegony* was here adapting an original local version whereby Odysseus settled and died in this part of the world. The internal logic of the relevant story-pattern demands this: it is a familiar motif that a hero is told to settle (? permanently) wherever he observes such and such a phenomenon (compare, for instance, Cadmus' founding of Thebes on the site where a cow came to rest). In *Od.* 11.134ff. Tiresias prophetically announces to Odysseus that he will have a death *ex halos*, a phrase whose original signification (see below, p. 90f.) was probably 'away from the sea': such a detail is considerably more appropriate to death among the Thesprotians than to death in the island of Ithaca. Finally, the very end of Apollodorus' *Epitome* supplies a neat parallel for what is envisaged: a local tradition that the exiled Odysseus died in Aetolia having married the princess there, by whom he had a son.

A further slight mitigation of the *Telegony*'s treatment concerns sheer practicalities: for the plot of the epic to reach its climax, Telegonus, Odysseus' son by Circe, has to grow up and reach manhood. Odysseus must be given something to do while his son is growing up, and the next sentence of Proclus' résumé makes it clear that, rather than give its hero an inglorious old age on Ithaca, the *Telegony* preferred to revive some of the martial glories of the *Iliad*: war broke out between the Thesprotians and the Brygans and Odysseus took command of the former. In a battle Ares routed Odysseus and his troops and Athena intervened against him. Apollo separated the two deities. That the Thracian war-god should help a nearby tribe makes eminent good sense. The clash between him and Athena recalls their Iliadic hostility (5.850ff. and 21.418ff.); and Athena's intervention also reminds us of her support for her protégé *passim* in the *Odyssey*. How Apollo was an appropriate deity to part them is not so easy to see.

After the death of Callidice, rule over the kingdom was assumed by Polypoetes, Odysseus' son <by Callidice>, and the hero himself sailed back to Ithaca. At this point we may consider the evidence of F 1 where Pausanias attributes to a poem called the *Thesprotis* (see above, p. 85) the detail that on returning home from Troy Odysseus had a son Poliporthes by Penelope. This squares with Apollod. *Epit.* 7.35: when Callidice died, Odysseus handed the kingdom to his son and returning to Ithaca he discovered that Penelope had born to him Poliporthes. The proliferation of children is impressive to the point of absurdity, and quite at odds with the reserved treatment by the *Odyssey*, in which the birth of only one son in each generation of Odysseus' family is a significant fact (*Od.* 16.117ff.). More sons for Odysseus by Circe are credited at Hes. *Th.* 1011f.

Poliporthes' name is intended as a commemoration of his father's sack of Troy (it is almost identical with the epithet Odysseus bears at *Il.* 2.278). Compare the naming of Telemachus and Neoptolemus by reference to their father's participation in the Trojan War (above, p. 43). Similarly, in 'Hesiod' (fr. 221 MW), Telemachus fathers on Nestor's daughter Polycaste a boy named Persepolis after the city-sacking of both his grandfathers. (Odysseus, too, is said to be named after a characteristic of *his* grandfather's at *Od.* 19.405ff.)

The last and climactic episode of the poem, Odysseus' death at the hands of his son Telegonus, takes as its basis a very familiar story-telling motif, the final encounter between a long-parted father and son, whose failure to recognise each other leads to the death of one. The tale of Sohrab and Rustum, for instance, provides a mirror-image of the device as used in the *Telegony*. Apollodorus' *Epitome* 7.36-37 presents a slightly fuller account of our story, and several of its additional details may be traceable back to the *Telegony*.

For instance, where Proclus merely says that Telegonus set out by sea in search of his father, put in at Ithaca and began ravaging the land, Apollod. *Epit.* 7.36 specifies that Telegonus began raiding the cattle. Other details in late authors may likewise derive from our epic. Thus Hyginus *Fab.* 127 adds that Telegonus was driven to Ithaca by a storm. And the second century AD poet Oppian in his work on fishing (*Halieutica* 2.497ff.) explains that, on setting out, Telegonus received from his mother Circe the very weapon which was to kill Odysseus.

Of that actual death all Proclus' résumé has to report is that Odysseus sallied out to deal with the stranger who was ravaging his kingdom, and was slain by his son, who failed to realise his father's identity. It is Apollodorus who makes clear what must have originally been stated in our epic: that the rather odd weapon wielded by Telegonus against his father was a spear barbed with the spine of a sting-ray (cf. Oppian as cited above). This strange detail represents an attempt to re-interpret Tiresias' prophecy to Odysseus in the *Nekyia* (*Od.* 11.134ff.). There Odysseus is guaranteed a death when he is very old: the death will be gentle or soft and *ex halos*. As we saw above (p. 88) this last phrase must originally have signified 'away, far from, the sea', a promise that the wanderings and dangers which had marred Odysseus' homecoming would be a thing of the past. The *Telegony*'s poet has altered the significance of the words (as the *Cypria*'s poet gave a new twist to 'the will of Zeus' mentioned in the *Iliad*'s proem: see above, p. 34) so that Odysseus' death comes (with his son Telegonus) 'from [or out of] the sea.' The deadly wound inflicted by a barb from a sting-ray can hardly be termed gentle, and the *Telegony* presumably twisted the *Odyssey*'s words still further in a new (and perverse) direction by detecting in them an allusion to the soft flesh of the sting-ray.

The sequel to Odysseus' death as given by Proclus is that Telegonus recognised his mistake and brought his father's corpse, together with Telemachus and Penelope, back to his mother Circe. Apollod. *Epit.* 7.37 mentions a lament by Telegonus. The notorious final sentence of Proclus' summary revealing the dénouement of the last poem within the Epic Cycle, has evoked pity and contempt in about equal proportions: Circe made them all immortal; Telegonus married Penelope, Telemachus married Circe. This is a second-rate Greek epic's equivalent of 'they all lived happily ever after'. The detail is confirmed by F 2. A scholion on Lycophron's *Alexandra* 805 claims the tradition of a resurrected Odysseus, but any such detail (which may be an *ad hoc* invention) could have had no place in our epic, where Penelope must be symmetrically paired off to Telegonus. (It is true that the unemended text of F 2 mentions *Calypso* as the mother of Telegonus *or* Teledamus but this is surely an author's slip caused by the (correct) mention of

Calypso in the immediately preceding sentence. We should follow those scholars who rewrite to make *Circe* mother by Odysseus of Telegonus *and* Teledamus rather than suppose an unattested tradition of Calypso resurrecting, immortalising and marrying Odysseus.) Odysseus was presumably buried on Circe's island. Hyginus *Fab.* 127 states that the double marriage which scholars have found so droll took place *monitu Minervae.* Apollod. *Epit.* 7.37 has the further detail that Telegonus and Penelope were sent by Circe to the Isles of the Blessed, a locale for specially favoured heroes from sixth-century poetry onwards. Perhaps this too derives from our epic; either way we are presumably to infer for this fuller version that Telemachus and Circe remain behind on the latter's island. It is hardly necessary to stress the intensely unHomeric nature of all this. The frivolous ease with which the boundaries between human and divine (so crucial for Homeric epic) are broken down is extraordinary, though all too typical of the Epic Cycle.

Index of Mythological Names

(Only the most important names and occurrences are listed)

Acamas 75
Achilles 42-58 *passim*, 64, 78
Adrastus 27
Aegaeon 15
Aeneas 47, 70, 71f., 76
Aeson 81
Aethra 69, 75
Agamedes 86
Agamemnon 41, 44f., 63, 69, 75, 77ff.
Ajax *Locrian* 72f., 78f.
Ajax *Telamonian* 56ff., 61ff., 73f.
Amphiaraus 25ff.
Andromache 69f., 73
Anius 45
Antilochus 53f., 56
Aphareus, *sons of* 39ff.
Aphrodite 36f., 40, 46
Apollo 52, 55, 88
Ares 51, 88
Arion 27
Artemis 44, 47, 52
Astyanax 69, 73f.
Athena 26, 35, 63, 66, 71ff., 77, 88
Augeas 85
Briseis 47
Calchas 42, 44, 73, 77f.
Callidice 88f.

Capaneus 26
Cassandra 38, 68, 72f., 80
Castor 36ff.
Chiron 16f., 35
Chryseis 47
Circe 90f.
Creon 19
Cronus 13, 17
Cycnus 46
Deidameia 43
Deiphobus 64, 72
Demophon 69, 75
Diomedes 48f., 63, 66ff., 77
Eos 53ff.,
Epeius 66
Epopeus 41
Eriphyle 27
Eris 35
Eteocles 23, 25
Eurydice 49
Euryganeia 20f.
Eurypylus 63, 65
Gê 13f.
Gorgons 49
Graces 36
Haemon 19
Hector 46
Helen 36f., 39, 46, 64, 66, 69

Index of Mythological Names

Helenus 38, 63
Helios 15
Hephaestus 35, 53
Hera 34f., 40
Heracles 41
Hermes 35
Hesperides 17f.
Hilaeira 39
'Hundred-Handers' 14
Iphianassa 44
Iphigenia 44f.
Iris 41
Laocoon 71
Leda 38
Leto 52
Lycaon 47
Machaon 63, 74
Manto 30
Medea 81
Melanippus 26
Memnon 53ff., 57, 65
Menelaus 39, 41f., 46, 63f., 69, 77, 80
Menestheus 69, 75
Nauplius 80
Neoptolemus 43, 64f., 68f., 73, 79
Nestor 41, 53f., 61f., 77
Odysseus 42f., 46, 48f., 52, 56ff., 61ff., 66ff., 73, 79, 84-91 *passim*
Oedipus 19ff., 23ff., 41
Palamedes 16, 42, 48, 80
Paris 35ff., 64
Parthenopaeus 26
Patroclus 47

Peleus 35, 43, 79
Penelope 88ff.
Penthesileia 51f.
Philoctetes 45, 63, 68
Philyra 17
Phoebe 39
Phoenix 43, 79
Pleisthenes 39
Poliporthes 89
Polydeuces 36ff.
Polyneices 23ff., 42
Polypoetes 89
Polyxena 49, 73
Polyxenus 85f.
Podalirius 74
Pontus 14
Poseidon 27, 73f.
Priam 68, 71f.
Protesilaus 46
Tantalus 82f.
Telegonus 88ff.
Telemachus 42, 89ff.
Telephus 42, 44, 65
Themis 34
Thersites 52
Theseus 39, 41, 69
Thetis 34f., 37f., 46, 53f., 56f., 79
Thoas 66
Tiresias 30, 78, 87f., 90
Titans 13ff.
Tithonus 53
Troilus 47
Trophonius 86
Tydeus 26, 28
Uranus 14
Zeus 13, 15f., 33ff., 37f., 49, 82

Lightning Source UK Ltd.
Milton Keynes UK
UKOW06f0605040216

267672UK00001B/125/P